THE VERTICAL AI A.U.T.O.B.O.T.™

Building AI Agents for Business Growth

CHETAN JOSHI

Author

Chetan Joshi

Title

The Vertical AI A.U.T.O.B.O.T.™

ISBN

978-1-917815-16-1

Category

Technology – Business – Management

Publisher

Breakfree Forever Publishing

Design By

RarePixels Design LLP

Limits of liability/disclaimer of warranty

The author and publisher of this book have used their best efforts in preparing this material. The author and publisher make no representation or warranties with respect to the accuracy, applicability or completeness of the contents. They disclaim any warranties (expressed or implied), or merchantability for any particular purpose. The author and publisher shall in no event be held liable for any loss or other damages, including (but not limited to) special, incidental, consequential or other damages. The information presented in this publication is compiled from sources believed to be accurate. However, the publisher assumes no responsibility for errors or omissions. The information in this publication is not intended to replace or substitute professional advice. The author and publisher specifically disclaim any liability, loss, or risk that is incurred as a consequence, directly or indirectly, of the use and application of any of the contents of this work. Printed in the United Kingdom.

Dedication

This book is dedicated to my wife, **Swati**, and my son, **Tanay**.

Thank you for standing by me during one of the most significant pivots of my professional life, from management consulting into the world of artificial intelligence. Your patience, belief, and quiet encouragement gave me the confidence to step away from what was familiar and build something new. None of this would exist without your support.

To my parents **Narendra** and **Nayna**, thank you for your unwavering belief in me over the years. Your values, resilience, and constant encouragement have shaped how I approach both work and life, and I carry that foundation into everything I build.

A special thank you to **Har Pulak Bahadur & Anita Coggins**, whose depth of thinking and practical leadership in Vertical AI fundamentally shaped my understanding of Automation, Control, and Intelligence. Much of the thinking in this book has been refined through learning how real, production-grade AI systems are designed and deployed.

I am also grateful to **Andy Harrington** for helping me turn experience, ideas, and structure into a clear and actionable playbook that leaders can genuinely use.

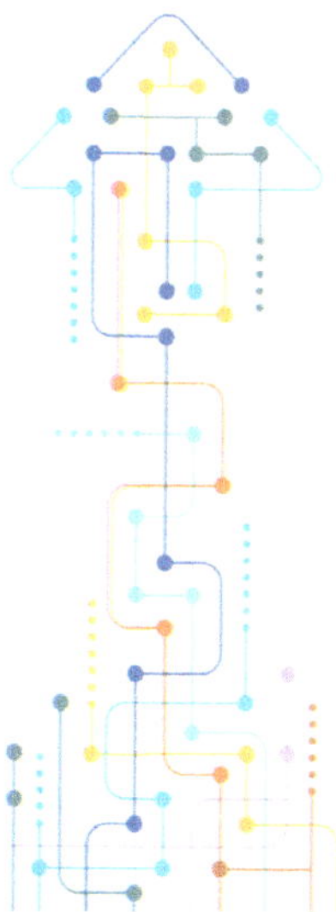

My thanks to **Sunil Kara**, who taught me the core design principles behind building high converting websites and mobile applications, with a relentless focus on user experience (UX) and user interface (UI). That discipline strongly influences how I think about building AI systems that are intuitive, trusted, and adopted in the real world.

Table of Contents

Introduction

From AI Noise To AI Confidence

> Innovation is saying no to a thousand things.
>
> ***- Steve Jobs***

Every business leader I meet today carries the same quiet tension.

They know artificial intelligence matters. They know it is no longer optional. They know it will shape the future of their organisation in ways that are difficult to predict but impossible to ignore.

Most have already begun. Pilots are underway. Tools are being tested. Teams are experimenting.

And yet almost every conversation ends in the same place.

Hesitation

Not because leaders lack ambition. Not because they lack intelligence. But because they lack confidence.

AI looks powerful. It sounds transformative. The demonstrations are impressive. But when the conversation turns to accountability, to regulation, to operational risk, something shifts. The excitement gives way to caution.

In high-stakes environments, confidence is everything. Without it, decisions stall. Responsibility blurs. AI becomes something that is discussed in strategy decks rather than embedded in daily operations. It becomes theatre instead of transformation.

This book exists for leaders who are tired of theatre. Tired of hype cycles. Tired of glossy demos that cannot survive real operational pressure.

Tired of asking, "**But can we trust it?**"

It is written for those who want clarity rather than confusion. Systems rather than slides. Outcomes they can defend to regulators, boards, and clients.

This is not a book about playing with AI.
It is a book about building it properly.

This playbook is based on real deployments across regulated financial institutions and growth-stage businesses, where accuracy, control, and accountability are not optional.

This is not a book about experimentation.

It is a blueprint for measurable transformation.

When applied with discipline, **the Vertical AI A.U.T.O.B.O.T.™** playbook enables organisations to:

- Reduce operational exception volumes by up to 40% by embedding deterministic intelligence into repetitive workflows
- Move AI agents from pilot to controlled production in under 90 days through staged architectural design

- Replace 25–35% of repetitive execution safely, without increasing regulatory exposure
- Free senior judgement capacity by eliminating mechanical decision layers
- Increase decision velocity while strengthening auditability and traceability

These are not vanity metrics.

They are the natural outcomes of combining Automation, Control, and Intelligence in the correct order.

This is production architecture.

It is about moving from noise to confidence. From experimentation to execution. From curiosity to capability. From zero to hero in Vertical AI.

The Two Babies Problem

To understand why so many AI initiatives falter, we need to simplify the conversation.

Imagine two babies born on the same day.

The first is raised on the entire world. It hears every language, sees every image, and absorbs every idea. Over time, it becomes expressive and imaginative. It can discuss almost anything. It can generate stories, summaries, designs, and possibilities. It is creative. It is impressive. It is artistic.

But it does not understand your organisation.

→ It does not know your rules.
→ It does not recognise your risks.
→ It does not carry your regulatory burden.

This is what most people today call AI **Generative AI Horizontal AI.** It is extraordinary at exploration and communication. But it was not designed to execute your business processes.

Now imagine the second baby.

This one grows up inside your organisation. It learns only your workflows. It understands your data structures. It is trained on your controls, your compliance obligations, and your definitions of success and failure.

It does not improvise. It does not speculate. It performs.

Consistently. Predictably. Within defined boundaries.

This is Vertical AI

The mistake most organisations make is not adopting AI It is confusing these two forms of intelligence.

When **Generative AI hallucinates**, produces inconsistent results, or fails under operational scrutiny, leaders conclude that "**AI does not work for our business.**"

The truth is simpler.

The wrong intelligence was given the wrong job.

This book exists to ensure that mistake is not repeated at scale.

Where Most Organisations Stand

Across industries, the pattern is remarkably consistent.

Some organisations are experimenting enthusiastically but cautiously. The tools feel helpful at first. Productivity appears to increase. But when outputs must be explained, audited, or defended, uncertainty creeps in. Errors are difficult to trace. Confidence erodes.

Others remain largely manual. Critical workflows depend on spreadsheets, inboxes, shared drives, and heroic individuals who "**just know how things work.**" This feels safer than automation. Yet it introduces delays, hidden fragility, and operational risk that only becomes visible during stress.

Many leaders are simply stuck. They sense the opportunity. They recognise the urgency. But the path forward feels unclear. Teams are unsure what AI means for their roles. Accountability appears ambiguous. Decisions are postponed not because the need is doubtful, but because the consequences feel uncertain.

If this sounds familiar, you are not behind.

You are normal.

But normal is becoming expensive.

Despite differences in geography and sector, the underlying objectives are remarkably similar.

Leaders want AI they can trust.

They want systems that are accurate by design, not accurate by luck. They want scale without burning out their teams. They want visibility without micromanagement. They want control without suffocating bureaucracy.

Above all, they want **100% confidence**.

Confidence that when an AI agent executes a workflow, it does so correctly. Confidence that when a regulator asks a question, there is an answer. Confidence that intelligence enhances judgement rather than undermines it.

These outcomes do not emerge from copying trends or bolting on tools.

They emerge from architecture.

They emerge from discipline.

They emerge from building AI the same way **we build human capability: deliberately and in stages.**

The principle that Underpins Every Reliable AI System

There is a temptation in AI to prioritise intelligence. To leap toward prediction, optimisation, transformation.

But capability is layered.

If the foundations are unstable, confidence never forms.

Every reliable AI system is governed by three forces:

Automation. Control. Intelligence.

Automation removes repetitive effort from humans.

Control ensures every action is traceable, auditable, and defensible.

Intelligence surfaces insight at the moment decisions are made.

Remove any one of these, and the system becomes fragile.

→ Automation without control creates risk.
→ Control without intelligence creates bureaucracy.
→ Intelligence without automation creates noise.

Vertical AI works because it balances all three.

→ It does not replace humans. It strengthens them.
→ It does not remove accountability. It reinforces it.
→ It does not introduce chaos. It introduces clarity.

This balance is what turns AI from an experiment into an operating capability.

From Zero to Hero in Vertical AI.

This book will not teach you how to "use AI tools."

It will teach you how to **design and build AI agents** that **operate inside your business.**

→ You will learn where Generative AI belongs and where it does not.
→ You will learn how to define a workflow precisely enough for intelligence to execute it.
→ You will understand how to embed control from day one rather than retrofit it after a failure.

Most importantly, you will build confidence step by step.

By the end, you will no longer ask whether AI can be trusted.

→ You will know where it belongs.
→ You will know how to build it.
→ You will know how to scale it responsibly.

You will move from reacting to AI change to architecting it. **From AI noise to AI confidence.**

Your First Step Begins Now

As you progress through this book, you will notice something deliberate.

Every chapter asks you questions.

Not abstract reflections. Not motivational prompts.

Practical questions

→ What exact workflow are you targeting?
→ What decision must be executed flawlessly?
→ What controls must never be breached?
→ What outcome defines success?

These questions are not academic. They are architectural.

By answering them, you will determine whether a Vertical AI agent should exist in your business, and what it should do.

And those answers will form the foundation of your first critical asset:

A.U.T.O. → Pilot → Blueprint → Build → Production

This becomes your A.U.T.O. Pilot Blueprint, your foundation for building an AI agent properly.

To support this, I have created a structured **A.U.T.O. Pilot Blueprint that captures** the key decisions required to design your first Vertical AI workflow.

Scan the QR code to begin building your Vertical AI Playbook: coglateral.ai/ai-start.

If this is unclear, you are not ready to build

an AI agent.

What Happens Next

When you scan the QR code, you will be guided through your A.U.T.O. Pilot.

You will:

- → Define your workflows, outcomes, and control points
- → Progress through each stage of the A.U.T.O. framework
- → Move from idea to a validated, production-ready blueprint

This is not a form.

It is a system designed to take you from thinking to execution.

That is how architecture becomes an advantage.

Start Your Vertical AI Transformation Here

This is where most AI initiatives succeed or fail.

Reading creates awareness.
Building creates confidence.
And confidence is what turns AI from an idea into an advantage.

Welcome The Vertical AI A.U.T.O.B.O.T.™ Playbook.

This is not a theoretical guide.

By the end of this book, you will have:

- → Defined a high-impact Vertical AI use case aligned to your business
- → Designed a controlled, production-ready workflow
- → Captured your A.U.T.O. Pilot Blueprint
- → Identified key risks, controls, and decisions
- → Created a clear execution path from idea to deployment

You will move from AI noise to AI confidence.

Now we begin...

Chapter 01

From Human Robot To Vertical AI Architect

“

The best way to predict the future is to invent it.

- Alan Kay

I entered investment banking as a securities lending graduate analyst in July 1997.

From my very first day, I was trained to operate like a precise component inside a much larger machine. Accuracy mattered. Deadlines were unforgiving. Mistakes carried real consequences, not just commercially, but personally and professionally.

This was not advisory work.

It was an operational reality under pressure.

In those early years, technology looked very different. Email technically existed, but it was slow and unreliable. The internet was not embedded into daily workflows. We stood in front of large white fax machines sending critical financial data one page at a time. Errors were corrected with Tippex (a small pot and a brush of white paint). Sensitive information was copied onto floppy disks and sent by post to counterparties, often taking days to arrive, only to be questioned and resent.

That was normal.

Looking back, I describe that phase of my career as **living like a human robot.**

Highly capable people, me included, sacrificed evenings, weekends, friendships, and health in pursuit of performance metrics and progression. I worked twelve-hour days clicking the same buttons, reconciling the same breaks, hearing the same system alerts on repeat.

The work itself was not unintelligent.

The problem was that intelligent humans were being consumed by repetitive, rules-based execution that should never have required human intervention in the first place. Judgement was being spent on mechanics rather than decisions. Experience was being drained by the process.

Figure 1: The Human Robot Trap

Highly capable humans are consumed by repetitive tasks rather than by judgement and decision-making.

Figure 1 represents more than an illustration. It represents a design flaw that still exists in thousands of organisations today.

The issue was never effort. It was architecture.

By 2006, at the age of twenty-nine, the cost of that architecture became impossible to ignore.

There was a moment I remember clearly.

It was late on a Friday night. Well past 9pm.

Markets had been volatile all day. Breaks were piling up. A reconciliation that should have taken minutes was stretching into hours. My screens were filled with numbers. My inbox was out of control. My manager was asking for status updates.

And I remember thinking:

This system does not need me. It needs redesigning.

The exhaustion was not from effort.

It was from knowing that intelligent people were being used to compensate for poor architecture.

That was the moment I stopped wanting a promotion. And started wanting change.

On paper, my career looked successful. Inside, I was exhausted. Burnt out. I felt trapped inside inefficient systems that demanded everything from me while giving very little back.

I was often the hardest worker in the room.

And I was losing myself in the process.

So, I walked away.

To most people around me, the decision made little sense. I retrained as a masseuse and reflexologist. It was not a strategic pivot. It was survival. I needed to slow down, reset, and reconnect with what it meant to help people rather than constantly firefighting problems created by broken systems.

Working with the human body taught me something no technology role ever had.

When stress, tension, and imbalance are ignored for long enough, something eventually breaks.

The same is true for organisations.

That pause reshaped how I saw work, people, and progress.

I learned that working harder is not the same as working smarter. That busyness often masks poor design. That care, trust, and clarity are not soft extras. They are structural foundations.

When I eventually returned to financial services and technology, I carried those lessons with me.

I no longer wanted to be the human glue holding inefficient systems together.

I wanted to redesign the systems themselves.

From Execution To Design

Over the following decades, technology advanced rapidly. Connectivity improved. Systems became faster. Yet organisations continued to exhaust their people to compensate for fragile process design and legacy thinking.

After the Global Financial Crisis, scrutiny intensified. Regulation tightened. Controls became mandatory. Transparency was no longer optional. Processes that once relied on trust or informal workarounds were suddenly expected to be explainable, auditable, and defensible.

Manual processes were exposed as fragile. Legacy systems struggled to adapt. Teams were asked to do more with less, while the cost of errors increased dramatically.

Once again, humans were compensating for systems that had never been designed to cope with complexity or scale.

My role began to shift.

I moved from executing processes to redesigning them. From operating inside systems to questioning why those systems existed in the first place. From keeping things running to fixing what was broken.

That shift required understanding where automation genuinely helps and where it introduces risk. Where intelligence adds value and where it creates noise. Where control must tighten and where flexibility must expand.

It required learning the difference between technology theatre and operational reality.

The Moment AI Became Practical

In 2024, artificial intelligence matured beyond hype and headlines for me.

For the first time, I could design systems that genuinely handle repetitive execution without sacrificing control. Not generic intelligence, but domain-specific intelligence. Not surface-level automation, but embedded operational capability.

This was not about replacing people.

It was about protecting their judgement.

It was about moving humans out of mechanical repetition and into strategic decision-making.

That insight led me to pivot fully into **Vertical AI**.

Conversations changed. Doors opened. I began working with banks, hedge funds, founders, and small businesses who all shared a common goal. They wanted growth without burnout. Control without bureaucracy. Scalability without fragility.

They did not want another tool.

They wanted architectural change.

Why This Book Exists

This book is not about chasing AI trends.

It is about helping you move from zero to architect.

You do not need to be a data scientist. You do not need to write code. You do not need a PhD in machine learning.

You need clarity.

You need structure.

You need a playbook that translates operational pain into intelligent design.

The Vertical A.U.T.O.B.O.T.™ playbook was built from lived experience across three decades of regulated environments, operational pressure, and technology transformation. It is designed to help you:

- Identify where human judgement is being wasted
- Redesign processes intelligently
- Build domain-specific AI agents
- Protect governance and control
- Scale growth without sacrificing people

This is not theoretical.

It is production-tested thinking.

Repetition steals human judgement long before it steals time.

If you want to build AI agents for business growth, you must first understand why they are necessary. And you must see clearly where your current design is leaking energy, talent, and opportunity.

Chapter Reflection

"The problem was never the people. It was the system they were forced to become."

Take ten minutes and answer honestly:

→ Where in your organisation are intelligent people compensating for broken systems?
→ Which repetitive tasks consume judgement that should be reserved for decisions?
→ If those tasks disappeared tomorrow, what higher-value work could your people focus on instead?

Write down one process that drains energy but adds little strategic value.

That process is where your AI journey begins.

In the next chapter, we move from personal history to clarity.

Before you build an AI agent, you must understand what kind of intelligence you are working with.

Because not all AI is designed to do the same job.

And misunderstanding that difference is where most organisations go wrong.

This section contributes directly to your A.U.T.O. Pilot Blueprint, helping you apply the right type of AI to the right business problem.

Capture this clearly in your **A.U.T.O. Pilot Blueprint**. These decisions will form the foundation of your production-ready AI design.

Chapter 02

Two Kinds of AI

Why Generative AI and Vertical AI Are Different and Why Both Matter

> A computer is incredibly fast, accurate, and stupid. Humans are incredibly slow, inaccurate, and brilliant. Together they are powerful beyond imagination.
>
> ***- Albert Einstein***

When **ChatGPT** entered living rooms in late 2022, artificial intelligence stopped being theoretical.

It stopped being a research paper.
It stopped being a vendor slide.
It became personal.

Leaders began experimenting.
Students began learning differently.
Boards began asking urgent questions.

Excitement grew quickly.
So did fear.

And in the rush, something important was misunderstood.

Most organisations began their AI journey using the wrong type of intelligence for the wrong job.

That confusion still explains why so many AI pilots fail.

If you want to go from zero to hero in AI and if you want to build **AI agents** that genuinely grow your business rather than create risk. You must first understand one foundational truth:

There are two fundamentally different kinds of AI

And they are not interchangeable.

What Is an AI Agent?

An AI agent is a system that can perceive, decide, and act within a defined business workflow to achieve a specific outcome.

Unlike traditional automation, which follows fixed rules, or generative AI, which produces content, an AI agent operates with purpose. It does not just respond. It executes.

In a business context, an AI agent typically:

→ Receives inputs from structured or unstructured data sources

→ Applies logic, models, and controls to make a decision

→ Takes action within a system or workflow

→ Produces a measurable, auditable outcome

For example:

→ A reconciliation agent that matches trades and flags exceptions

→ A client onboarding agent that validates documents and triggers approvals

→ A revenue operations agent that qualifies leads and routes them intelligently

Within the Vertical AI A.U.T.O.B.O.T.™ framework, an AI agent is not just a model.

It is a controlled system embedded inside a real business process.

This distinction matters;

Because businesses do not scale from insights alone. They scale from **execution.**

The Two Babies

To simplify the noise, imagine two babies.

Both are intelligent.
Both can learn.
But they grow up in completely different environments.

The First Baby: Generative AI (Horizontal AI)

The first baby is raised on the entire world.

It absorbs language, images, stories, opinions, patterns, and creativity from everywhere. Over time, it becomes expressive, articulate, imaginative.

This is Generative AI (Gen AI).

It is powered by Large Language Models (LLMs). These models are trained on vast, general datasets drawn from across the internet and public knowledge.

Generative AI is **probabilistic** by design. Its answers are likely, not certain.

It excels at:

→ Explaining ideas
→ Summarising information
→ Drafting content
→ Brainstorming possibilities
→ Translating between contexts

It supports thinking.

But it does not execute your regulated workflows.
It does not understand your operating model.
It does not naturally respect your internal controls.

This is not a flaw.
It is simply not what it was built for.

The Second Baby: Vertical AI (Narrow AI)

The second baby grows up inside your world.

It learns only what matters:

→ Your workflows.
→ Your data structures.
→ Your controls.
→ Your regulatory obligations.
→ Your definition of success.

This is Vertical AI (VAI).

It operates through what I refer to as Large Domain Models (LDMs).

An LDM does not learn from the world.
It learns from your world.

Vertical AI is not creative.
It is scientific.
It is deterministic.
It performs.

It is designed to:

- Execute specific tasks accurately
- Produce consistent, auditable outcomes

Operate within defined boundaries

Reduce operational risk

It supports doing.

In a bank, that might mean reconciling trades, validating collateral movements, flagging threshold breaches before escalation, or automating margin workflows.

In a founder-led business, it might automate onboarding, invoicing, fulfilment, compliance checks, or customer communications without introducing inconsistency.

Vertical AI does not improvise.

It executes.

The Confusion at The Heart of AI Adoption

When generative AI went mainstream, many leaders assumed it was the long-awaited breakthrough.

After years of:

→ Outsourcing programmes
→ Rule-based engines
→ Macros layered on macros
→ Robotic process automation that fractured under edge
cases organisations hoped this was finally "real AI".

Early outputs looked impressive.

Then **hallucinations** appeared.

Accuracy slipped.

Edge cases broke confidence. And boards concluded:

"AI doesn't work for us."

The problem was not AI

The problem was using artistic intelligence where scientific intelligence was required.

When It Truly Clicked for Me

I first encountered the concept of Vertical AI in 2019 in a highly regulated banking environment.

What struck me was not the terminology.

It was the results.

Focused, domain-specific pilots produced measurable ROI (Return On Investment) almost immediately. Real workflows stabilised. Risk reduced. Exception noise dropped. Humans were freed to apply judgement rather than chase operational errors.

That moment shifted my career.

I realised consulting around broken processes was no longer enough.

The future was building intelligent systems inside them.

Years later, when generative AI exploded into public consciousness, I finally had the language to explain what I had seen.

We were confusing two different forms of intelligence.

How The Two Should Work Together

This is not a choice.
In mature AI architectures:

Vertical AI produces the truth.
Generative AI communicates it.

The LDM remains the source of record.
The LLM becomes the interface.

One ensures accuracy.
The other ensures usability.

One controls execution.
The other supports interpretation.

When combined properly, you gain automation without losing trust.

This is the foundation of the Vertical AI A.U.T.O.B.O.T.™ playbook you will build throughout this book.

If you want to become an AI architect rather than an AI experimenter, this distinction is non-negotiable.

From Zero To Hero in AI

Most people approach AI backwards.

They start with tools.

They experiment with prompts.

They test chatbots.

They chase novelty.

Heroes build differently.

They begin with:

→ A defined workflow
→ Clear controls
→ Measurable outcomes
→ Deterministic execution

They design the Vertical AI first.

Then they layer generative intelligence on top.

This is how you move from curiosity to capability.
From automation theatre to operational leverage.
From AI noise to AI confidence.

Chapter Reflection

"AI does not fail under pressure. It exposes where the wrong intelligence was trusted."

This section contributes directly to your A.U.T.O. Pilot Blueprint, helping you apply the right type of AI to the right business problem.

Capture this clearly in your **A.U.T.O. Pilot Blueprint**. These decisions will form the foundation of your production-ready AI design.

Ask yourself:

→ Where is AI currently being asked to replace judgement rather than support it?
→ Which workflows in your business require certainty rather than creativity?

→ Where would accuracy, control, and auditability create immediate confidence?
→ Write down one process where precision matters more than speed.

That is where your first Vertical AI agent belongs.

Now that the difference between artistic intelligence and scientific intelligence is clear, the next question becomes unavoidable:

Why do so many AI initiatives still collapse under real operational pressure?

That is where we go next.

Chapter 03

Why Most AI Pilots Fail

> You don't scale chaos. You eliminate it.
>
> ***- Andy Grove***

The Green Dashboard Trap

Automation promises speed.
Artificial intelligence promises scale.

Together, they are sold as transformation.

Deploy a model.
Connect some data.
Reduce cost.
Increase throughput.

But automation without control is one of the fastest ways to introduce invisible risk into a business.

I have seen it in global banks.
In ambitious FinTech platforms.
In scaling founder-led companies.

The technology changes.
The ambition grows.
The slide decks improve.

The pattern remains.

Early excitement.
Quick wins.
Then fragility.

Not dramatic failure.

Quiet erosion.

Where Most AI Pilots Go Wrong

AI pilots rarely fail because artificial intelligence does not work.

They fail because organisations begin with the wrong intelligence.

Generative AI is inserted directly into operational workflows. It summarises. It classifies. It drafts. It recommends.

The outputs look impressive.

Until they are not.

Accuracy fluctuates.
Edge cases multiply.
Hallucinations appear.
Decisions cannot be reproduced consistently.

Trust fractures. Leaders do not say, "**We misapplied probabilistic intelligence.**"

They say, "**AI doesn't work for us.**"

But **generative AI is probabilistic by nature**. It predicts likely answers. It is expressive and exploratory.

Operational systems require determinism.
They require traceability.
They require accountability.

Expecting artistic intelligence to behave like a compliance engine is not innovation.

It is misplacement.

And misplacement is expensive.

The Illusion of Quick Wins

Automation creates movement.

Movement is often mistaken for progress.

A painful process is identified.
A tool is deployed.
Early metrics improve.

Turnaround times accelerate.
Manual effort drops.
Dashboards glow green.

But governance remains untouched.

Controls are not redesigned.
Accountability is unclear.
Escalation paths are vague.

The system works when conditions are stable.

Production is not stable. I remember one volatility event where trade volumes surged dramatically in less than 48 hours.

What had looked like a stable AI-assisted reconciliation pilot suddenly faced three times its normal load.

Edge cases multiplied. Data timing shifted. Exception queues swelled. Nothing was technically broken.

But the system had never been stress-tested under real pressure. Within a week, manual controls were quietly reintroduced "just to be safe."

That is how AI dies. Not in failure. In doubt.

Under scale, volatility, or scrutiny, fragility surfaces.

Automation without governance becomes amplified risk.

Why AI Pilots Collapse In Production

Pilots are forgiving.

Production is not.

In production, AI faces real clients.
Real money.
Real regulators.
Real consequences.

Most pilots are designed to demonstrate possibility.

They are not engineered to survive scrutiny.

When audit asks for lineage, answers are incomplete.
When regulators request evidence, it is fragmented.
When volatility increases, errors propagate faster.

Without control, confidence disappears.

When confidence disappears, systems are switched off.

Not because AI failed.

Because architecture failed.

A Corporate And Fintech Example

Inside banks and FinTech platforms, uncontrolled automation does not fail loudly.

It drifts.

AI-driven reconciliation or exception tools perform well during pilots. Then volumes increase. Market volatility rises. Edge cases multiply.

Thresholds drift.
Exceptions misclassify.
Decision trails fragment.

Dashboards remain green.

When internal audit asks how decisions were made, explanations are partial.

When regulators demand defensibility, governance gaps appear.

The technology did not fail.

The operating model did.

Automation was introduced without redesigning control.

In high-trust industries, that gap is costly.

A Founder And SME Example

The same pattern appears in small to medium-sized enterprises (SME).

A founder automates onboarding, invoicing, fulfilment, lead routing, or customer service.

Throughput improves.
Costs fall.
The team feels relief.

Then pressure arrives.

A supplier fails.
A customer dispute escalates.
A data inconsistency spreads.

No one knows where the source of truth lives.

The CRM says one thing.
The accounting system says another.
The automation platform executes actions no one fully understands.

Spreadsheets return.
Firefighting resumes.
Momentum slows.

Automation was meant to create freedom.

Instead, it created fragility.

The issue is not automation.

It is automation without control.

Control is The Price of Trust

Trust is not an emotion.

It is engineered.

Every AI system that deserves to scale must integrate three forces:

- → **Automation.**
- → **Control.**
- → **Intelligence.**

Automation creates efficiency.
Control creates safety.
Intelligence creates visibility.

Remove control and automation becomes liability.
Remove intelligence and control becomes bureaucracy.
Remove automation and scale disappears.

Most AI pilots fail because they optimise speed before they secure safety.

And speed without safety is exposure.

The Real Lesson

Automation without control does not fail loudly.

It fails quietly.

Until the cost becomes unavoidable.

The question is not whether AI works.

The question is whether it is designed to survive reality.

Chapter Reflection

"Technology does not create trust. Architecture does."

This section contributes directly to your A.U.T.O. Pilot Blueprint, helping you apply the right type of AI to the right business problem.

Capture this clearly in your A.U.T.O. Pilot Blueprint. These decisions will form the foundation of your production-ready AI design.

Pause and reflect:

→ Where has automation created movement without clarity?
→ Which processes only work when conditions are stable?
→ What automated decision today would you struggle to defend under scrutiny?

That is your risk signal.

Eliminate chaos before you scale it.

That is how AI moves from experiment to infrastructure. That is how pilots become production.

That is how you win.

When AI is designed with control first, outcomes compound.

Exception queues shrink.

Manual overrides fall.

Escalation noise drops.

In properly architected environments, **operational exception volumes routinely reduce by 30–40%** within the first structured deployment cycle.

The difference is not intelligence. **It is design.**

Chapter 04

The Hidden Cost of AI Mistakes

> Risk comes from not knowing what you're doing.
>
> ***- Warren Buffett***

The cost of getting AI wrong is rarely immediate.

It does not usually arrive as a dramatic system failure or public scandal. It accumulates quietly. It spreads across risk, finance, people, and reputation until the damage becomes unavoidable.

By the time leaders recognise it, momentum has already been lost.

This is what makes AI mistakes so dangerous. Not because they are spectacular. But because they are subtle.

Most organisations underestimate this cost because it does not appear neatly on a balance sheet. It shows up in delayed reconciliations. In inconsistent decisions. In rising exception queues. In strained teams. In subtle loss of trust.

And by the time it is visible, advantage has already shifted elsewhere.

AI introduced without control does not fail loudly. It erodes quietly.

Regulatory Exposure

In regulated industries, accountability does not disappear because technology is involved.

Regulators do not accept "**the system did it**" as an explanation. When AI decisions cannot be explained, traced, or justified, responsibility remains firmly with the organisation.

I have seen firms deploy automation, believing it reduces risk, only to discover, under scrutiny, that they cannot answer basic questions:

- Why did the system make this decision?
- Who approved the logic?
- What data was used at the time?
- What controls were in place?

In one institution, an AI-assisted classification workflow had been running quietly for months.

Performance metrics looked stable.

Then an internal audit request arrived.
The team was asked to demonstrate why a specific exception had been classified as low risk rather than escalated.

The model output could be shown.
But the reasoning path could not.

For several days, senior leadership sat in uncomfortable silence as teams reconstructed decision logic in retrospectively.

Nothing catastrophic happened.
But confidence shook.
Not because the AI failed.
Because explainability had not been designed from day one. That week changed how the organisation viewed automation. Control stopped being optional.

Even when operations or technology are outsourced, accountability never leaves. Governance does not transfer with the supplier. Regulatory scrutiny does not relocate.

As expectations increase, tolerance for opaque decision-making decreases.

AI must be designed with auditability from the outset.

Control is not optional.

It is expected.

Financial Leakage

Poorly governed AI leaks value.

Not all at once.
Not dramatically.
But consistently.

Errors compound. Exceptions are handled inconsistently. Humans spend time correcting machine output instead of eliminating root causes. Refunds increase. Rework becomes routine.

Early dashboards may show speed.
They rarely show instability.

This is one of the most dangerous myths in AI adoption:

If it looks faster, it must be better.

Speed without accuracy creates rework.
Scale without control creates leakage.

Margins erode not because demand falls, but because execution becomes unstable.

Vertical AI exists to prevent this. It embeds intelligence and governance directly into workflows so that accuracy precedes scale.

Efficiency without control is an illusion.

Talent Attrition

People do not leave organisations because AI exists.

They leave because uncertainty exists.

When systems behave unpredictably, confidence erodes. When automation feels imposed rather than designed, fear replaces curiosity. Roles become ambiguous. Accountability becomes unclear.

High performers want leverage.
They do not want chaos.

I have watched talented individuals disengage not because they feared replacement, but because they no longer trusted the systems, they were asked to rely on.

Knowledge walks out quietly. Morale declines. Institutional memory thins.

AI introduced without clarity weakens culture instead of strengthening it.

If your best people spend their time fixing automation rather than improving outcomes, something has gone wrong in the design.

Reputation Damage

Trust, once lost, is expensive to rebuild.

Clients expect accuracy.
Partners expect reliability.
Markets expect resilience.

Failures caused by uncontrolled automation do not look innovative. They look careless.

In a world where information travels instantly, reputational damage spreads faster than remediation efforts can respond. One visible failure can undo years of credibility.

This is why confidence matters more than speed.

You can recover from being late.

It is far harder to recover from being wrong.

Why Waiting is Not Neutral

Faced with these risks, many leaders delay.

It feels prudent.
It feels cautious.

It is neither.

While some organisations hesitate, others move deliberately. They redesign workflows. They embed control. They build intelligence that survives scrutiny.

AI maturity compounds.

Those who move with discipline build advantage. Those who wait inherit urgency.

Waiting does not preserve the status quo. It widens the gap.

The Need For A Playbook

The lesson from failed pilots, regulatory exposure, financial leakage, talent loss, and reputational damage is clear.

AI cannot be treated as a technology experiment.

It is an operating model decision.

The question is not whether AI belongs in your organisation. The question is how to design it, so it delivers accuracy, control, and confidence at scale.

That is why this book exists.

AI mistakes rarely announce themselves.

They accumulate quietly until trust disappears.

This playbook exists to ensure that never happens.

Chapter Reflection

"The most expensive AI mistakes are the ones no one notices."

Pause and reflect honestly:

→ Where would an AI error cause the greatest damage in
your organisation?
→ Which decisions must be explainable under pressure, not merely correct most of the time?
→ What would happen to trust if those systems failed quietly for six months?

Write down one workflow where the cost of being wrong is higher than the cost of being slow.

That is where discipline must come before speed.

This section contributes directly to your A.U.T.O. Pilot Blueprint, helping you apply the right type of AI to the right business problem.

Capture this clearly in your **A.U.T.O. Pilot Blueprint**. These decisions will form the foundation of your production-ready AI design. Most AI initiatives fail not because of ambition, but because of a lack of structure and control.

So far, we have examined what goes wrong.

From the next chapter onward, we begin building what works.

Chapter Five is where The Vertical AI A.U.T.O.B.O.T.™ starts to take practical shape.

Now we move from risk… to architecture.

Chapter 05

A = Automate

> Automation applied to an efficient operation will magnify the efficiency. Automation applied to an inefficient operation will magnify the inefficiency.
>
> ***- Bill Gates***

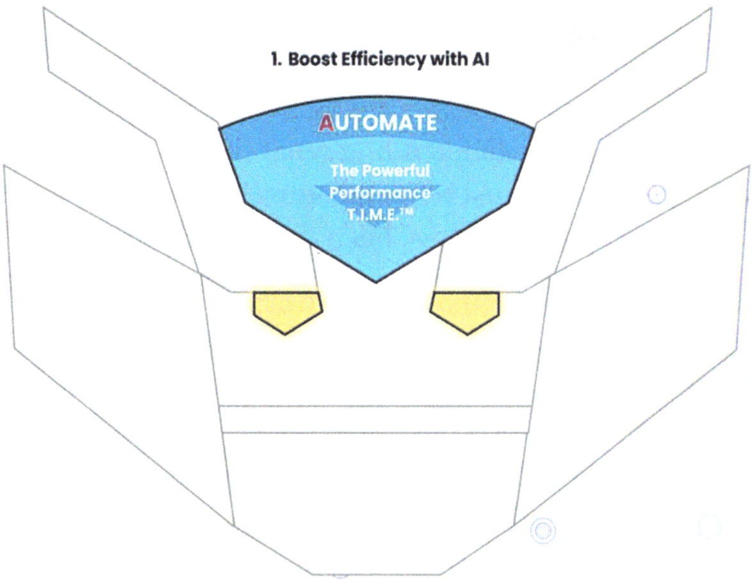

Up to this point, we have focused on why AI fails.

From here onward, the focus shifts to how it succeeds.

Every effective AI journey begins with one simple, practical question:

Where are Humans doing Work That Machines Should Already Be Doing?

Automation is where most organisations begin their AI journey.

It feels logical.
It feels safe.
It feels measurable.

Remove repetitive tasks. Save time. Reduce cost.

And yet, this is also where many initiatives quietly fail.

Not because automation is wrong, but because it is often applied without understanding what should be automated, what must remain controlled, and what humans should never have been doing in the first place.

I have spent decades inside organisations watching highly capable people perform the same steps, press the same buttons, and reconcile the same breaks day after day. Not because those tasks required judgement, but because no system had been designed to take responsibility for them.

Automation, done properly, is not about speed. It is about **freeing judgement**.

The purpose of **AUTOMATE** is simple: To remove repetitive, deterministic work from humans so they can focus on decisions, exceptions, and leadership.

This is not about replacing people.

It is about protecting them from work that slowly drains energy, attention, and confidence.

Why Automation Comes First

Most organisations already know where their pain lives.

It lives in repetition.
In re-keying the same data across systems.
In reconciling numbers that should already agree.
In approvals that exist only because systems do not trust one another.

These are not judgement-based activities.
They are executing work.

And execution work consumes human capacity at scale.

AUTOMATE comes first in the Vertical AI A.U.T.O.B.O.T.™ playbook because it creates immediate clarity. It exposes process weaknesses, data gaps, and control failures early, when they are cheapest to fix.

Done correctly, automation builds confidence.
Done badly, it amplifies chaos.

Automation is Not About Speed

One of the most common mistakes I see C-Suite & MDs make is assuming automation is about speed.

Speed is a by-product.

The real purpose of automation is **consistency**.

Vertical AI automation removes variability from tasks that should behave the same way every time. It allows humans to step back from mechanical execution and refocus on judgement, oversight, and decision-making.

This is not about replacing people.
It is about protecting them.

Why You will See Two Examples From Here on

From this chapter onward, each pillar of the playbook is illustrated through two practical examples.

This is deliberate.

Over the years, I have worked across four types of organisations, often at very different stages of maturity, but facing the same underlying challenge: how to scale intelligently without exhausting people or increasing risk.

These groups include large corporates, particularly in Banking and Financial Services, Financial Technology firms building platforms and products, founders leading fast-growing businesses, and small to medium-sized enterprises (SME) scaling with limited resources.

While their language, constraints, and scale differ, the patterns do not.

Repetition overwhelms people.
Trust in systems erodes.

Growth introduces fragility.
Judgement gets buried under execution.

To make this playbook genuinely useful, each pillar is therefore shown through two lenses:

A Corporate & FinTech Example, where scale, regulation, and accountability are dominant forces.
A Founder and SME Example, where time, confidence, and control are often the scarcest resources.
The purpose is not comparison, but transferability.

The principles in this book are designed to scale up, scale down, and adapt to context. Whether you are operating a global institution, building a FinTech product, or growing a business yourself, the same questions apply:

- → What should humans really be doing?
- → What work should never have required them in the first place?
- → And how do we build AI that earns trust rather than creates risk?

With that framing in place, we begin where every sustainable AI journey must begin.

By removing repetition.

A Corporate And Fintech Example

In the Banking and Financial Services, reconciliation is a classic candidate for automation.

Historically, highly capable teams have spent hours each day matching trades, positions, and balances across systems. During periods of volatility, volumes increase, exceptions multiply, and pressure rises.

I have seen institutions attempt to address this through headcount, outsourcing, or rigid rule-based engines. None of these approaches removes risk. They simply redistribute it.

When Vertical AI agents are introduced, the approach changes.

Repetitive matching is automated.
Breaks are classified intelligently.
Only genuine exceptions are surfaced to humans.

Judgement is applied where it matters, not where it is wasted.

The result is not just faster processing. It is a calmer operation.

A Founder And SME Example

For founders and growing businesses, automation often starts with invoicing, onboarding, or order processing.

In one business I worked with, the founder personally approved every invoice. Not because they wanted control, but because previous errors had damaged trust.

Growth stalled. Not due to lack of demand, but due to lack of confidence in the systems.

Vertical AI automation introduced clear validation, rules, and exception handling. The founder remained in control without being trapped in execution.

Automation restored trust.

But before that shift, there was tension. The founder had reached the point where growth no longer felt exciting. It felt heavy. Revenue was rising. But so were mistakes.

So were late nights. So was the constant checking.
One evening, they said something that stuck with me:
"I built this to create freedom. Why does it feel like it owns me?"
That is what broken automation does.

It traps intelligent people inside processes that should never have required them.

When the workflow was stabilised and exceptions dropped by over 30%, something changed that no dashboard captured. The founder stopped hovering. And started leading again.

The Powerful Performance T.I.M.E.™

Automation within the Vertical AI A.U.T.O.B.O.T.™ playbook is governed by **The Powerful Performance T.I.M.E™** model.

My clients learn these four skill areas which ensures automation delivers value without introducing new risk.

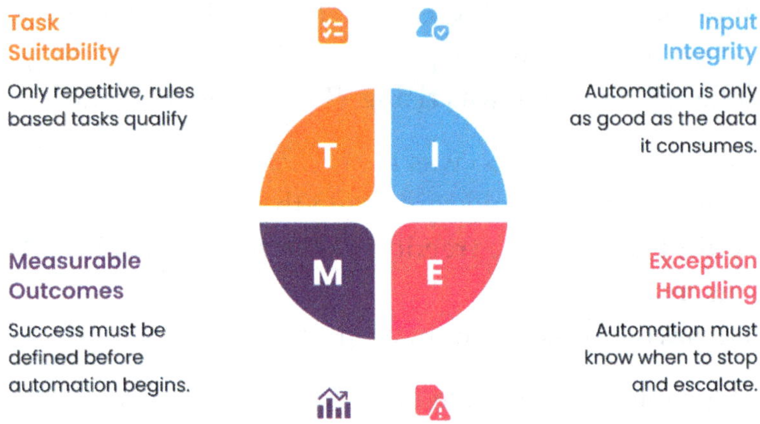

The Powerful Performance T.I.M.E.™ model prevents automation hype.

It replaces hope with evidence.

Figure 2: The AUTOMATE Layer

Removing repetitive execution so humans can focus on judgement and decision-making.

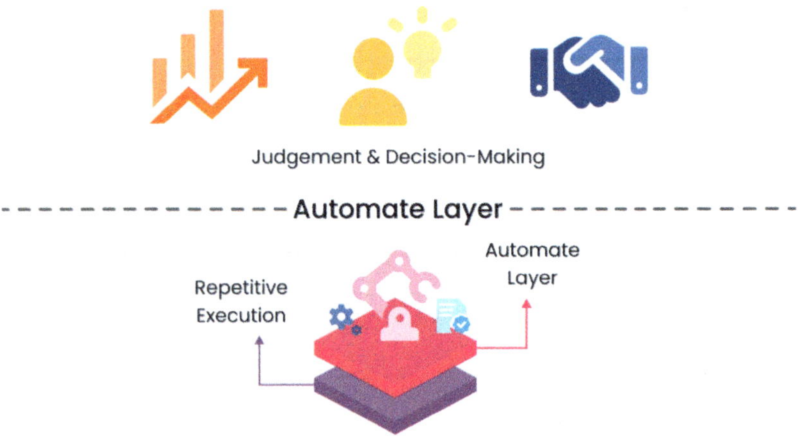

Automate As Part of The A.U.T.O. Pilot

Automation alone does not create intelligence.

This is why it sits inside the A.U.T.O. Pilot phase:

- **AUTOMATE** proves repetition can be removed
- **UNRAVEL** proves data can be trusted
- **TRAIN** proves accuracy can be achieved
- **OPTIMISE** proves performance can scale

Only when all four are satisfied should systems move into production. This is the difference between pilots that impress and systems that endure.

Chapter Reflection

"Repetition steals human judgement long before it steals time."

A.U.T.O.B.O.T. Assembly Progress: Piece 1 of 7
You are now installing Piece 1 of your Vertical AI A.U.T.O.B.O.T.™.

1 2 3 4 5 6 7

This piece removes repetition without losing control. Your A.U.T.O.B.O.T.™ is now taking shape.

This section contributes directly to your A.U.T.O. Pilot Blueprint, helping you apply the right type of AI to the right business problem.

Capture this clearly in your **A.U.T.O. Pilot Blueprint**. These decisions will form the foundation of your production-ready AI design.

At this stage, most organisations realise that building an AI agent is not about the model. It is about how it connects, operates, and scales within existing systems.

Reflect honestly:

- → Where in your organisation are people repeating tasks that require no judgement?
- → Which activities exist only because systems cannot handle them reliably?
- → What work would immediately improve morale if it was removed from human hands?

Write down one process that feels safe to automate first.

That process is your AUTOMATE anchor.

Automation removes friction.

But friction often hides something deeper.

Before AI can be trusted, data must be understood.

That is where we go next.

UNRAVEL.

Chapter 06

U = Unravel

> Without data, you're just another person with an opinion.
>
> ***- W. Edwards Deming***

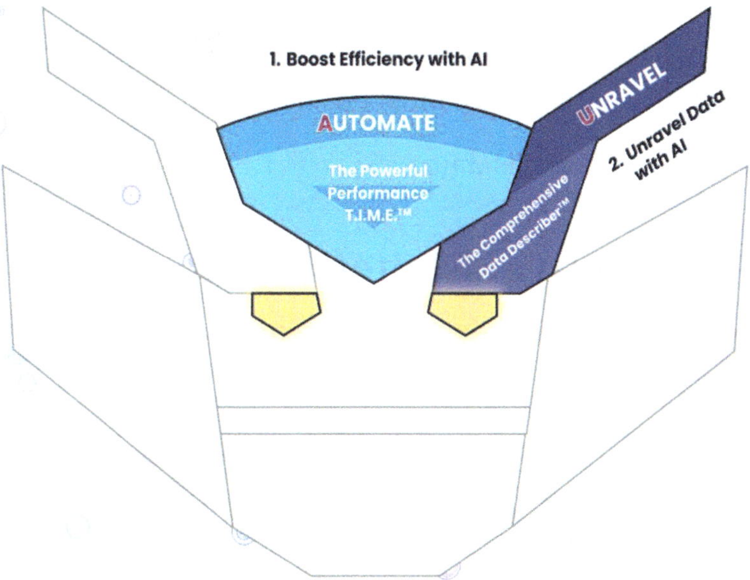

Up to this point, automation has removed repetition.

But automation alone is not enough.

Because once humans step back from execution, a deeper problem is exposed.

Data.

Not missing data.
Not big data.
But untrusted data.

Every AI system, no matter how advanced, is constrained by one simple truth:

AI can only be as reliable as the data it understands.

This is why UNRAVEL comes immediately after AUTOMATE.

Before AI can be trained, optimised, or trusted, the raw material of intelligence must be stabilised.

That raw material is data.

Why Unravel Matters

Most organisations do not suffer from a lack of data.

They suffer from fragmentation.

Information arrives in emails, PDFs, spreadsheets, chat tools, portals, images, and legacy systems. Each source contains a partial truth. No single source owns the whole story.

Humans compensate by interpreting, reconciling, and guessing.

That guessing is where risk begins.

UNRAVEL exists to remove interpretation from places it does not belong.

Its purpose is simple:

To turn fragmented inputs into a trusted intelligence layer that AI can safely build upon.

A Corporate And Fintech Example

In corporate and financial technology firms, data rarely lives in one place.

Client information sits in CRMs. Transaction data lives in core platforms. Documents arrive via email, portals, PDFs, spreadsheets, and messaging tools. Each system holds part of the truth, but no single system owns it.

Historically, organisations attempted to manage this through data warehouses, reconciliation layers, or manual controls. Teams were asked to **"clean"** data downstream, often under time pressure, with incomplete context.

The result was predictable.

Inconsistent data.
Conflicting reports.
Escalations driven by uncertainty rather than risk.

I have seen regulated firms pass audits while still lacking confidence in their own numbers, because the effort required to trace data lineage was simply too high. When

Vertical AI is introduced at the **UNRAVEL** stage, the focus shifts upstream.

Instead of forcing humans to interpret fragmented inputs, Vertical AI captures data at source, collates it across formats, and applies controls immediately. Unstructured documents are parsed. Fields are normalised. Relationships are created explicitly.

Most importantly, the system records how it knows what it knows.

This changes everything.

Data stops being something teams argue about and becomes something they trust. Exceptions are clearer. Reports align. Decisions are made faster, not because people rush, but because confidence replaces doubt.

UNRAVEL does not make data perfect.

It makes data dependable.

A Founder And SME Example

For founders and small to medium-sized businesses, data problems feel different but are just as damaging.

Information is scattered across tools adopted at speed. Accounting software, e-commerce platforms, CRMs, inboxes, spreadsheets, and notes all hold fragments of the business story.

Founders often know the numbers "in their head" but struggle to trust what systems are telling them. Reports disagree. Forecasts feel fragile. Decisions are delayed or second-guessed.

In one growing business I worked with, the founder avoided delegating financial oversight because past reporting errors

had created anxiety. Growth created complexity, and complexity eroded trust.

UNRAVEL changed the dynamic.

Vertical AI was used to capture inputs consistently, collate data across tools, and apply simple controls that highlighted inconsistencies early. Instead of reacting to surprises, the founder began seeing issues forming in advance.

Confidence returned, not because the business became simpler, but because the data became clearer.

For founders, UNRAVEL is not about dashboards.

It is about sleeping better at night.

The Comprehensive Data Describer™ (CCC)

UNRAVEL within the Vertical AI A.U.T.O.B.O.T.™ playbook is governed by The Comprehensive Data Describer™ model built on three non-negotiables:

C – Capture All relevant data is captured at source, regardless of format.

C – Collate Data is structured, normalised, and connected across systems.

C – Controls Validation, lineage, and ownership are applied immediately.

My clients use these three skill areas (CCC) to ensure data becomes explainable, auditable, and trustworthy before AI relies on it.

This is how intelligence earns credibility.

Figure 3: From Data Chaos to Data Trust

Turning fragmented inputs into a trusted intelligence layer through capture, structure, and control

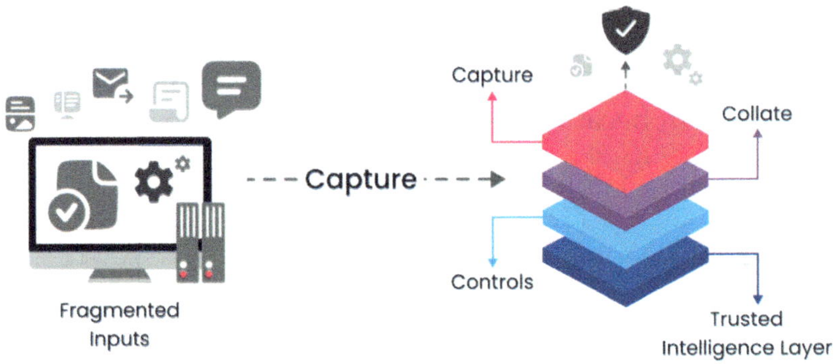

Unravel As Part of The A.U.T.O. Pilot

UNRAVEL does not exist in isolation.
It is the second proof point in the A.U.T.O. Pilot:

AUTOMATE proves repetition can be removed

UNRAVEL proves data can be trusted

TRAIN proves accuracy can be achieved

OPTIMISE proves performance can scale

Without UNRAVEL, AI systems guess.

With UNRAVEL, they know.

Chapter Reflection

"Untrusted data forces humans back into the loop long after automation promised relief."

A.U.T.O.B.O.T. Assembly Progress: Piece 2 of 7
You are now installing Piece 2 of your Vertical AI A.U.T.O.B.O.T.™.

1 2 3 4 5 6 7

This piece replaces uncertainty with trust.
Your A.U.T.O.B.O.T.™ is gaining clarity.

This section contributes directly to your A.U.T.O. Pilot Blueprint, helping you apply the right type of AI to the right business problem.

Capture this clearly in your A.U.T.O. Pilot Blueprint. These decisions will form the foundation of your production-ready AI design.

AI does not fail in development. It fails in operation, where scale, exceptions, and real-world behaviour expose weaknesses.

Reflect honestly:

- → Where does your organisation still rely on human interpretation to reconcile data?
- → Which reports create debate instead of clarity?
- → Where does a lack of data lineage slow decisions or increase anxiety?

Write down one data flow that feels fragile today.

That flow is your UNRAVEL anchor.

You have removed repetition.
You have begun to restore trust.

Now comes the moment that determines whether AI earns confidence or quietly loses it.

Accuracy.

That is where we go next.

TRAIN.

Chapter 07

T = Train

"

In God we trust. All others must bring data.

- W. Edwards Deming

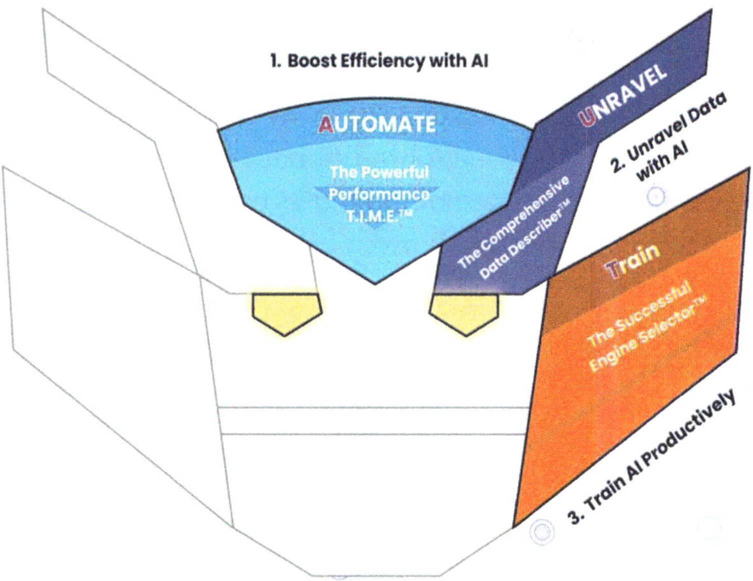

If automation removes repetition and data restores order, training is where confidence is either earned or quietly destroyed.

This is the point where many AI initiatives falter.

Not because the technology is weak.

But because training is rushed, improvised, or misunderstood.

I have seen organisations automate workflows and unravel data beautifully, only to lose trust the moment outputs become inconsistent. A single unexplained error can undo months of progress. Leaders stop listening. Teams override systems. Confidence leaks away.

Training is not a technical step.

It is a trust-building discipline.

When I first began working with production-grade Vertical AI, what struck me was how different the mindset was compared to traditional automation or rule engines. Training was not treated as experimentation. It was treated as accountability.

Every outcome mattered. "Every exception was examined.

Every failure was a signal, not an inconvenience.

That discipline changed everything.

Why Training is Where AI Earns Trust

Humans are remarkably forgiving of other humans.

We explain mistakes.
We apply context.
We give second chances.

Machines do not receive the same grace.

When AI gets something wrong, people don't just question the output. They question the system. And once confidence slips, recovery is difficult.

That is why Vertical AI training is designed around one principle:

Accuracy before scale.

Not speed.
Not coverage.
Not ambition.

Accuracy.

Training is where boundaries are defined. Where behaviour is shaped. Where the system learns what right looks like, not just what is likely.

This is where many organisations confuse generative intelligence with operational intelligence.

Generative AI can explore.
Vertical AI must perform.

A Corporate And Fintech Example

In corporate and FinTech environments, training is where trust is either earned or quietly lost.

I have seen institutions deploy AI models that looked impressive in controlled demos but failed under live conditions. Accuracy degraded when volumes spiked. Edge cases were missed. Outputs could not be explained clearly to risk teams or regulators.

The issue was never ambition.
It was discipline.

Training had been treated as a one-off event rather than a continuous, governed process.

When Vertical AI training is applied correctly, the mindset changes.

Training data is curated deliberately.
Edge cases are prioritised, not ignored.
Testing is performed against real operational scenarios, not idealised samples.

Most importantly, accuracy targets are defined before deployment, not excused after failure.

In one FinTech engagement, a Vertical AI agent was trained specifically to classify operational exceptions. Rather than aiming for generic accuracy, success was defined narrowly: near-perfect precision on high-risk categories.

The result was immediate.

- → Humans stopped second-guessing outputs.
- → Escalations reduced.
- → Confidence returned.

The AI was not trusted because it was intelligent. It was trusted because it was trained properly.

A Founder And SME Example

For founders and SMEs, training is often misunderstood as something only large organisations can afford.

In reality, poor training is far more dangerous for smaller businesses.

I worked with a founder who had implemented automation to triage customer enquiries. The system worked well most of the time, but when it failed, it failed publicly. Customers received incorrect responses. Confidence eroded quickly.

The problem was not automation.
It was training without testing.

When we re-approached the problem using Vertical AI principles, training became intentional.

The AI was trained on their customers.
Their language.
Their edge cases.

Accuracy was tested in quiet periods before being exposed at scale.

Once confidence was established, the founder stopped monitoring every interaction. Not because they stopped caring, but because the system had earned trust.

Training gave the founder something priceless:

Peace of mind.

The Successful Engine Selector™ (T.T.T.T)

Within the A.U.T.O.B.O.T.™ playbook, TRAIN is governed by a simple model "The Successful Engine Selector™" with a unforgiving discipline:

Triage. Tidying. Training. Testing.

- **Triage** Classify inputs and prioritise intelligently.
- **Tidying** Clean and standardise structured data
- **Training** Refine model behaviour within defined boundaries.
- **Testing** Validate performance under real-world scenarios

Skipping any one of these steps does not speed things up.

It simply moves risk downstream.

I have watched organisations celebrate early AI performance, only to see confidence collapse when market conditions change, volumes spike, or edge cases appear. The problem was never capability.

It was incomplete training.

Figure 4: From Data to Trust

Turning structured data into dependable intelligence through disciplined training and testing.

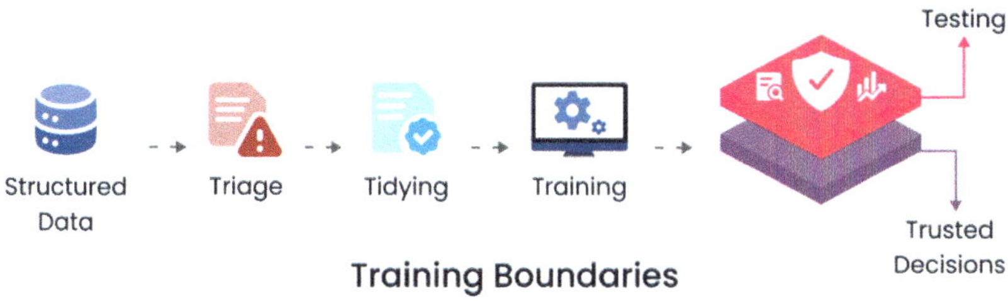

Train As Part Of The A.U.T.O. Pilot

TRAIN does not exist in isolation.

It is the third proof point in the A.U.T.O. Pilot:

→ AUTOMATE proves repetition can be removed
→ UNRAVEL proves data can be trusted
→ TRAIN proves accuracy can be achieved
→ OPTIMISE proves performance can scale

Without TRAIN, systems repeat mistakes.

With TRAIN, they improve.

What Training Changes For Humans

When AI is trained properly, something subtle shifts.

People stop checking outputs obsessively.
They stop second-guessing every recommendation.
They begin to rely on the system as a partner rather than a threat.

Judgement returns to where it belongs.

Not buried in mechanics but applied to decisions.

This is the moment where AI stops feeling experimental and starts feeling dependable.

And once trust appears, something else follows naturally. Performance.

Chapter Reflection

"AI earns trust the moment its behaviour becomes predictable under pressure."

A.U.T.O.B.O.T. Assembly Progress: Piece 3 of 7

You are now installing Piece 3 of your Vertical AI A.U.T.O.B.O.T.™.

This piece ensures your AI performs predictably under pressure.

This piece determines whether your system is tolerated or trusted.

Your A.U.T.O.B.O.T.™ is learning how to think.

This section contributes directly to your A.U.T.O. Pilot Blueprint, helping you apply the right type of AI to the right business problem.

Capture this clearly in your **A.U.T.O. Pilot Blueprint**. These decisions will form the foundation of your production-ready AI design.

At this point, the challenge is no longer understanding AI. It is executing it correctly, at scale, and with control.

Reflect honestly:

→ Where have past AI or automation efforts lost trust due to inconsistent outputs?
→ Which decisions in your organisation require certainty, not probability?
→ What would change if leaders trusted AI recommendations without constant human validation?

Write down one outcome where accuracy matters more than speed.

That outcome is your **TRAIN anchor**.

You have removed repetition.
You have begun to restore trust.

Now comes the moment that determines whether AI earns confidence or quietly loses it.

Accuracy.

That is where we go next.

OPTIMISE.

Chapter 08

O = Optimise

> What gets measured gets improved.
>
> ***- Peter Drucker***

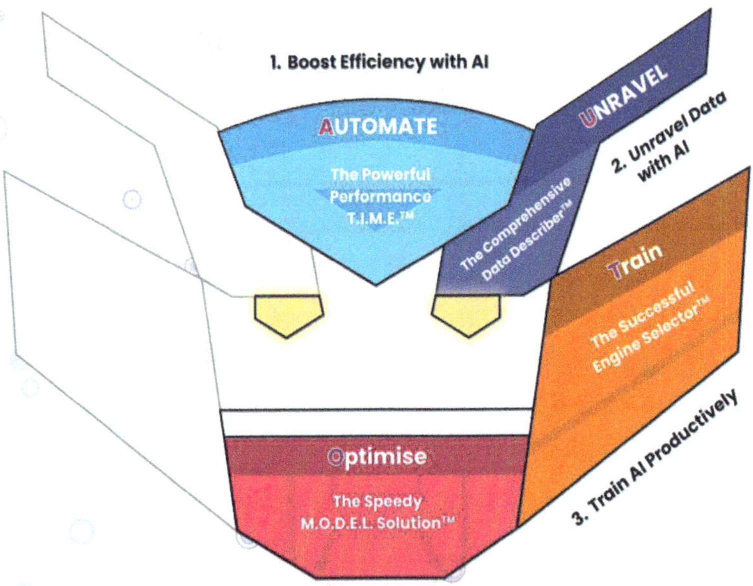

Optimisation is where many AI initiatives quietly break.

Not at the start.
Not during pilots.
But when success begins to scale.

Early results look promising. Accuracy improves.
Confidence grows. Usage increases.
And then, slowly at first, something changes.

Performance drifts.

In one case, performance degradation went unnoticed for months.

Accuracy had slipped from 99% to 94%.

At first glance, that looked acceptable.

But at scale, 5% drift meant hundreds of additional exceptions per week.

Teams began compensating manually.

Trust began eroding quietly.

No one blamed the model.

They blamed "AI."

Optimisation is not about squeezing more performance.

It is about preventing quiet decay.

Edge cases multiply.

Costs rise.

Trust weakens.

This is not failure.
This is unmanaged success.

OPTIMISE exists to ensure that as AI scales, it becomes **stronger**, not more fragile.

Why optimisation is Not About Speed

Most organisations misunderstand optimisation.

They treat it as acceleration.
More volume. More throughput. Morc output.

But true optimisation is about stability under pressure.

AI systems do not fail because they are slow.
They fail because they change.

Data shifts.
User behaviour evolves.
Business priorities move.
Regulatory expectations tighten.

Without continuous optimisation, even the most accurate AI quietly degrades.

OPTIMISE ensures performance is **observed, measured, and adjusted deliberately**, not discovered after damage is done.

The Speedy M.O.D.E.L. Solution™

Optimisation only works when it is systematic.

In the Vertical AI A.U.T.O.B.O.T.™ playbook, optimisation follows the "The Speedy M.O.D.E.L. Solution™" discipline:

- **M - Measure** performance continuously
- **O - Observe** behaviour and drift
- **D - Diagnose** root causes early
- **E - Enhance** deliberately, not reactively
- **L - Lock** improvements through control

Not through perfection.
Through predictability.

Figure 5: Optimisation Without Fragility

Maintaining stable performance at scale through continuous measurement and controlled improvement.

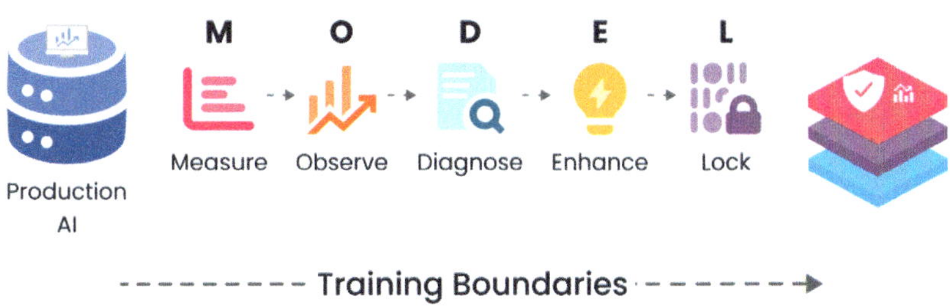

Optimise As Part Of The A.U.T.O. Pilot

Optimise does not exist in isolation

It is the fourth proof point in the A.U.T.O. Pilot:

- → A: AUTOMATE proves repetition can be removed
- → U: UNRAVEL proves data can be trusted
- → T: TRAIN proves accuracy can be achieved
- → O: OPTIMISE proves performance can scale

Without OPTIMISE, systems stall.

With Optimise, they evolve.

What Optimisation Looks Like in Practice

In corporate and FinTech environments, optimisation separates serious AI programmes from experiments.

Optimised AI:

- → Flags drift before it becomes visible to users
- → Improves accuracy without destabilising workflows
- → Evolves alongside the business rather than lagging behind it

Without optimisation, AI becomes brittle.
With optimisation, AI becomes dependable.

This is where AI stops being impressive and starts being trusted at scale.

Chapter Reflection

Scale does not break AI Unmeasured change does.

A.U.T.O.B.O.T. Assembly Progress: Piece 4 of 7

You are now installing Piece 4 of your Vertical AI A.U.T.O.B.O.T.™.

1 2 3 4 5 6 7

This piece ensures your AI remains reliable as success grows. Your A.U.T.O.B.O.T.™ is becoming dependable. This piece ensures your AI remains reliable as success grows.

AI remains reliable as success grows.

Your A.U.T.O.B.O.T.™ is becoming dependable.

This section contributes directly to your A.U.T.O. Pilot Blueprint, helping you apply the right type of AI to the right business problem.

Capture this clearly in your **A.U.T.O. Pilot Blueprint**. These decisions will form the foundation of your production-ready AI design. True value is not created from a single AI agent. It is created when that capability can be repeated, extended, and embedded across multiple workflows.

Reflect honestly:

→ Where could AI performance drift without being noticed today?

→ What metrics would reveal early warning signs, not just end results?
→ Who is accountable for improving AI after it goes live?

Write down one signal you are not currently measuring but should be.

That signal is your **OPTIMISE anchor**.

You have removed repetition.
You have structured data.

You have trained for accuracy.
You have stabilised performance.

Now comes the moment where AI leaves experimentation behind and enters the real world.

Production.

That is where we go next.

BUILD.

Chapter 09

B = Build

❝

Ideas are easy. Execution is everything.

- John Doerr

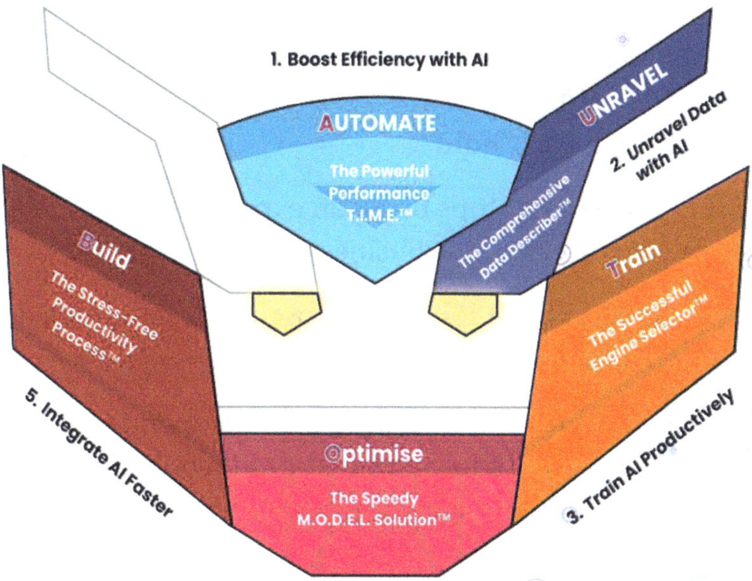

Most AI initiatives do not fail in the pilot.

They fail in the handover.

A pilot or proof of concept (PoC) runs well in isolation. A demo looks convincing. Early results feel promising. Then the real world arrives.

Volume increases.
Exceptions appear.
Stakeholders ask questions.
Governance gets involved.
Production teams inherit something they did not design.

This is the moment where confidence either hardens or collapses.

BUILD is about crossing that boundary deliberately.

Not rushing.
Not improvising.
Not hoping it will "**hold**".

BUILD is when AI stops being an experiment and becomes part of how the business actually works.

In organisations that follow this discipline, AI agents do not remain trapped in perpetual pilot.

They move a high-value, tightly defined operational workflow from pilot to controlled production in under 90 days, whether inside a regulated institution or a scaling founder-led business.

Not because corners are cut.

But because architecture was defined before code was written.

Why Pilots Rarely Survive Production

I have seen countless AI pilots stall at this stage.

Not because the model was wrong.
Not because the idea lacked value.

But because production realities were ignored.

- → Who owns the output?
- → Who intervenes when something breaks?
- → How are exceptions handled at scale?
- → What happens when inputs change?

Without clear answers, pilots become orphaned.

BUILD exists to prevent that.

Vertical AI is designed to move into production because it is built around **bounded responsibility, defined workflows, and clear operating rules from day one**.

You are not adding intelligence after the fact.
You are embedding it directly into the workflow.

Build is About Integration, Not Installation

Existing systems
Existing controls
Existing teams
Existing accountability

This is where many organisations hesitate.

They fear disruption.
They fear operational risk.
They fear regulatory exposure.

Ironically, the lack of structured integration poses the greatest risk.

When AI is bolted on, it becomes fragile.
When AI is integrated, it becomes dependable.

Figure 6: BUILD – From Pilot to Production

Integrating Vertical AI safely into live business workflows with ownership, controls, and accountability.

The Stress-Free Productivity Process™

BUILD within the Vertical AI A.U.T.O.B.O.T.™ playbook is governed by **The Stress-Free Productivity Process™.**

This skill area exists for one reason:

To ensure AI increases output **without increasing operational stress**.

The process focuses on **I.C.E.**

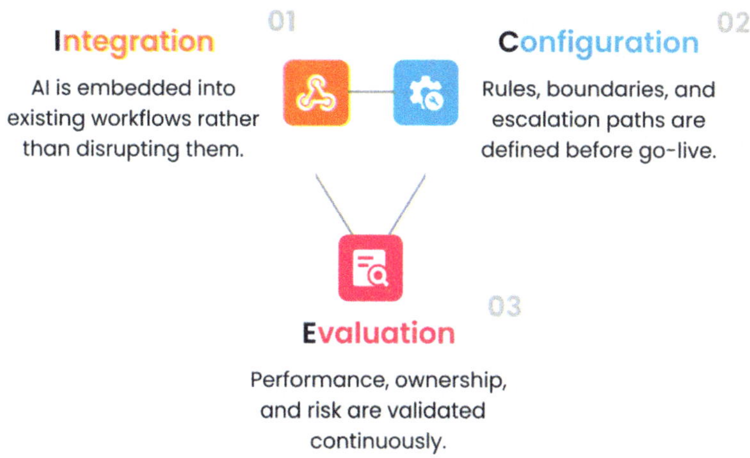

I.C.E ensures production AI does not feel brittle, noisy, or fragile.

It replaces anxiety with structure.

A Corporate And Fintech Example

In corporates and FinTech firms, the gap between pilot and production is often political as much as technical.

I have seen successful pilots stall because ownership was unclear. Technology teams delivered the model. Operations teams inherited the risk. Compliance teams arrived late.

Confidence evaporated.

When BUILD was approached by my clients through **The Stress-Free Productivity Process™**, the dynamic changed.

Integration was planned upfront.

The configuration included exception ownership and escalation. Evaluation was embedded into daily operations.

AI entered production quietly.

No drama.
No heroics.
No last-minute controls.

The system worked because responsibility was designed, not assumed.

A Founder And SME Example

For founders, BUILD is often where excitement turns into anxiety.

I worked with a growing business that had a successful AI pilot supporting customer onboarding. The founder loved the results but hesitated to fully deploy it.

"**What happens if it goes wrong?**" was the unspoken question.

BUILD created clarity.

The AI was integrated into existing tools.
Clear stop conditions were defined.
Human override remained explicit.

The founder did not lose control.

They gained confidence.

The system moved into production not because it was perfect, but because it was safe.

The Shift That Matters

When BUILD is done properly, something changes.

AI stops feeling experimental.
It starts feeling boring.

And that is a good thing.

Outputs stabilise.
Teams trust results.
Leadership gains visibility.

This is the moment AI becomes **operationally invisible and strategically valuable.**

Not because it is hidden.
But because it works.

Chapter Reflection

"Pilots prove possibility. Production proves responsibility."

A.U.T.O.B.O.T. Assembly Progress: Piece 5 of 7
You are now installing Piece 5 of your Vertical AI A.U.T.O.B.O.T.™.

This piece turns intelligence into dependable capability. Your A.U.T.O.B.O.T.™ is now becoming operational.

This piece turns intelligence into dependable capability.

Your A.U.T.O.B.O.T.™ is now becoming operational.

This section contributes directly to your A.U.T.O. Pilot Blueprint, helping you apply the right type of AI to the right business problem.

Capture this clearly in your **A.U.T.O. Pilot Blueprint**. These decisions will form the foundation of your production-ready AI design. AI investment is not justified by innovation. It is justified by measurable impact, sustained over time.

Reflect honestly:

Where do pilots currently stall in your organisation?
What prevents ideas from crossing into live production?
Who owns AI outcomes once they leave experimentation?

Write down one pilot that delivered value but never scaled.

That is your **BUILD anchor**.

You have removed repetition.
You have restored trust.
You have trained intelligence.
You have stabilised performance.

Now comes the discipline that keeps AI working day after day.

Governance.
Reliability.
Oversight.

That is where we go next.

OPERATE.

Chapter 10

O = Operate

> Systems run the world.
>
> **- *W. Edwards Deming***

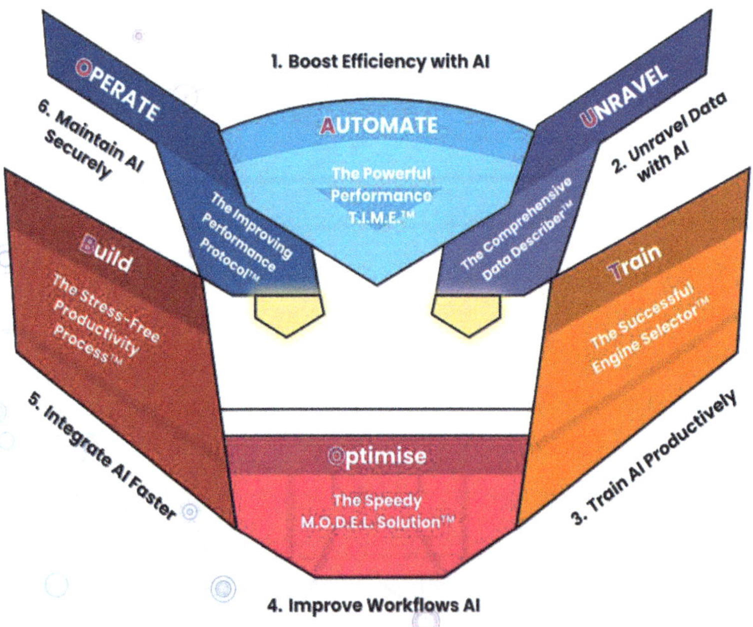

Most AI initiatives do not fail at launch.

They fail quietly, over time.

A model performs well at first.
Outputs look sensible.
Confidence builds.

Then conditions change.

Volumes increase.
Inputs shift.
Edge cases appear.
Human behaviour adapts around the system.

Nothing breaks dramatically.
But something weakens.

Trust.

OPERATE exists to prevent that erosion.

This chapter is about what happens after AI is live, when the excitement fades, and responsibility begins.

Because AI that cannot be operated safely cannot be trusted at scale.

Why Operate is Where AI Confidence is Won Or Lost

Many organisations assume AI performance is static.

They believe that once deployed, a system simply continues to work.

In reality, AI is a living capability.
It sits inside changing environments.

It processes evolving data.
It interacts with human decisions.

Without deliberate operational discipline, performance degrades quietly.

OPERATE is the discipline that keeps AI reliable, auditable, and defensible long after deployment.

This is where AI stops being a pilot project and becomes part of how the business actually runs in production.

The Improving Performance Protocol™

OPERATE within the Vertical AI A.U.T.O.B.O.T.™ playbook is governed by **The Improving Performance Protocol™.**

It exists to answer one critical question:

How do you keep AI trustworthy when no one is watching?

The protocol is built around four skill areas: S.S.S.S.

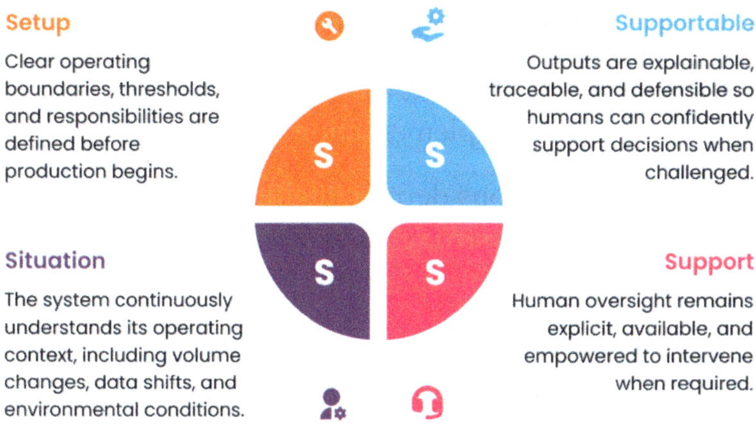

My clients use these four skill areas to ensure their AI never operates in isolation.

It remains part of a managed system, not a black box.

Figure 7: Operating AI as a System

Keeping AI reliable through monitoring, governance, and human oversight.

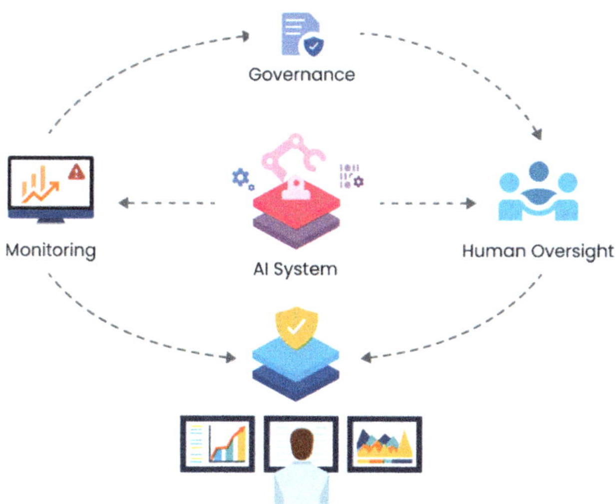

A Corporate And Fintech Example

In regulated environments, AI performance must survive scrutiny long after implementation.

I have seen institutions deploy intelligent automation successfully, only to struggle months later when regulators asked simple questions:

- → Why did this output occur?
- → Who approved the logic?
- → What controls were active at the time?

Without an operating protocol, answers were unclear.

When **The Improving Performance Protocol™** was applied, the change was immediate.

Operating metrics were visible.

Escalation paths were documented.
Human oversight was explicit.

The AI did not just work.

It could be explained.

That is the difference between operational success and reputational risk.

A Founder And SME Example

For founders and SMEs, **OPERATE** often determines whether AI becomes a trusted partner or an abandoned experiment.

I worked with a founder who initially loved their AI-driven workflow.

Over time, small inconsistencies appeared. Nothing dramatic, but enough to trigger doubt.

They stopped trusting the system.
Manual checks returned.
Efficiency quietly vanished.

Introducing **The Improving Performance Protocol™** restored confidence.

Clear thresholds were set.
Performance was reviewed regularly.
Human override was formalised, not ad hoc.

The founder stopped worrying.
The system stopped drifting.

AI became something they relied on, not something they monitored nervously.

Why OPERATE Comes Before TRANSFORM

Many leaders want to jump straight to transformation.

New roles.
New operating models.
New ways of working.

But transformation without operational confidence collapses under pressure.

OPERATE ensures AI is boring before it becomes bold.

Reliable before it becomes strategic.

This is what allows leadership to move from supervision to vision.

Chapter Reflection

"AI that cannot be explained cannot be trusted."

A.U.T.O.B.O.T. Assembly Progress: Piece 6 of 7

You are now installing Piece 6 of your Vertical AI A.U.T.O.B.O.T.™.

This piece ensures intelligence remains reliable over time. Your A.U.T.O.B.O.T.™ is now operating with control.

This piece keeps intelligence reliable over time.

This section contributes directly to your A.U.T.O. Pilot Blueprint, helping you apply the right type of AI to the right business problem.

Capture this clearly in your **A.U.T.O. Pilot Blueprint**. These decisions will form the foundation of your production-ready AI design.

Most AI strategies fail not in ambition, but in execution. Structure and discipline are what turn intent into results.

Reflect honestly:

→ Where could AI performance degrade without being noticed today

→ Which outputs would be hardest to explain under scrutiny

→ Where is human oversight assumed rather than designed

Write down one AI-driven process that needs clearer operating discipline.

That is your **OPERATE** anchor.

You have removed repetition.
You have restored trust.
You have trained intelligence.
You have stabilised performance.
You have embedded accountability.

Now comes the final step.

Leadership.
Change.
Direction.

That is where we go next.

TRANSFORM.

Chapter 11

T = Transform

> The biggest risk is not taking any risk.
>
> ***- Mark Zuckerberg***

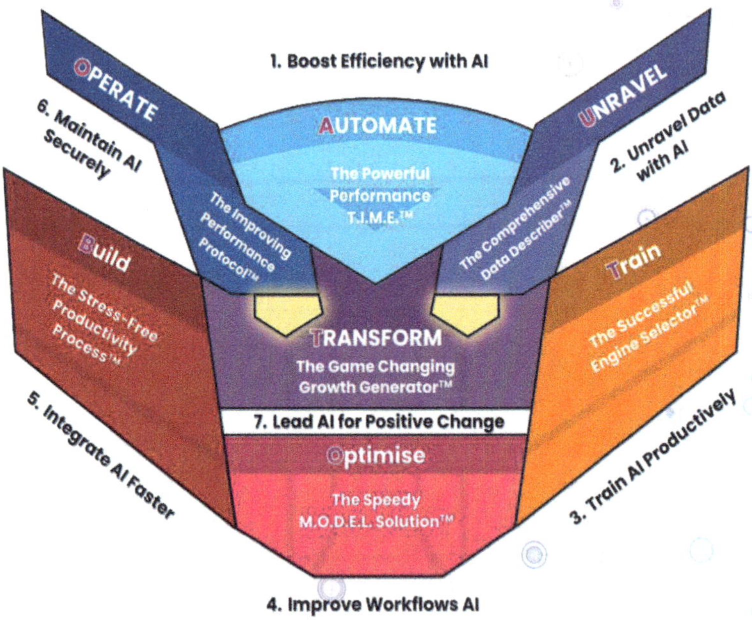

You are no longer exploring AI You are operationalising it.

By this stage, your Vertical AI A.U.T.O.B.O.T.™ is not an idea. It is a defined system ready for execution.

By this point, AI should no longer feel mysterious.

It should feel familiar.
Structured.
Manageable.

And yet, this is where many organisations still hesitate.

Not because the technology does not work.
But because leadership has not yet caught up to capability.

TRANSFORM is not a technical step.

It is a leadership one.

Why Transformation is The Hardest Step

Most organisations do not fail at automation, data, or models.

They fail at change.

AI introduces new ways of working.
New decision flows.
New definitions of responsibility.

And that makes people uncomfortable.

Teams worry about relevance.
Leaders worry about accountability.
Organisations worry about disruption.

So, AI is contained.

Pilots succeed.
Systems operate.
But behaviour stays the same.

TRANSFORM exists to prevent that outcome.

In the next five years, leadership will quietly split into two categories.

→ Those who supervise AI
→ And those who design with it.

Supervisors will remain reactive. Architects will become indispensable. The difference will not be intelligence. It will be courage to redesign.

AI will not replace leaders. It will expose whether they understand systems deeply enough to guide them.

Transformation is Not About Replacing Humans.

The greatest misconception about AI-led transformation is that it removes people.

In reality, it removes friction.

When AI handles execution, humans regain:

→ Judgement
→ Focus
→ Time

→ Confidence

TRANSFORM is about elevating human contribution, not diminishing it.

Leaders stop managing tasks and start managing outcomes. Teams stop reacting and start anticipating. Organisations stop firefighting and start designing.

This is the point where AI becomes a competitive advantage rather than a cost centre.

Figure 8: From Automation to Transformation

Moving from task execution to human-led decision-making through trusted AI systems.

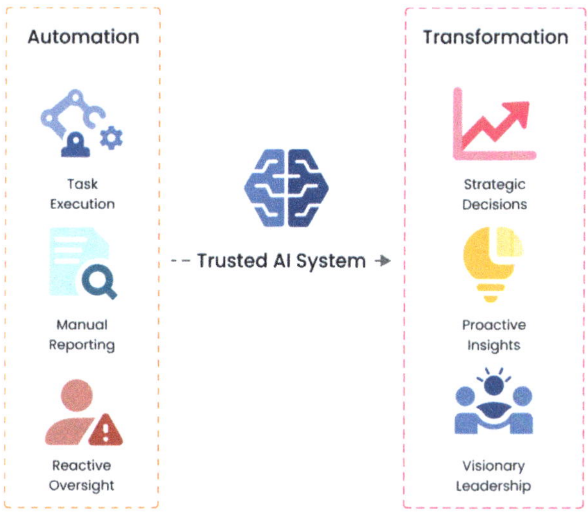

A Corporate And Fintech Example

In large Corporates, transformation often stalls because AI is seen as an operational tool rather than a leadership enabler.

I have worked with institutions where Vertical AI delivered stability, accuracy, and scale, yet leadership behaviour remained unchanged.

Decisions were still escalated unnecessarily. Reports were still manually reconciled.

Oversight was still reactive.

When leaders were shown how AI could surface insight proactively, something shifted.

Meetings changed. Risk conversations matured.

Confidence increased.

AI stopped being something teams explained upwards.

It became something leadership relied on.

That is transformation.

A Founder And SME Example

For founders, TRANSFORM often shows up as relief.

The constant pressure to be everywhere eases.
Decision bottlenecks dissolve.
The business stops depending on one person's memory or intuition.

I have seen founders regain weekends.
Sleep better.
Think more clearly.

Not because they worked less, but because systems worked better.

AI did not replace their vision.

It gave it room to breathe.

The Game Changing Growth Generator™

Transformation within the Vertical AI A.U.T.O.B.O.T.™ Playbook is governed by:

The Game Changing Growth Generator™

This is the structured discipline that ensures AI becomes a strategic advantage rather than a technical experiment.

It operates through the S.T.A.T. framework:

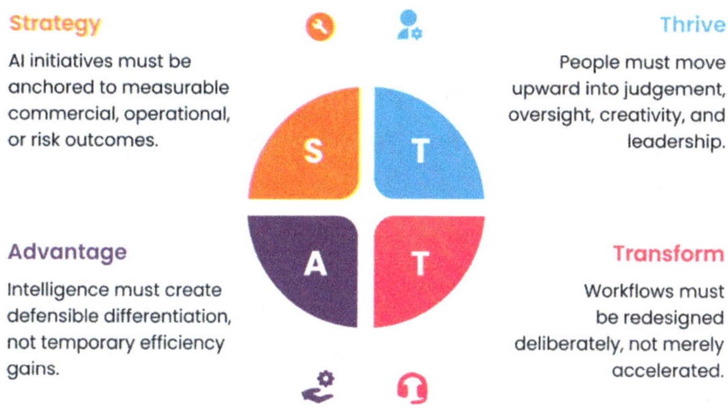

The Game Changing Growth Generator™ prevents organisations from mistaking activity for impact.

It ensures AI scales value, not just volume.

What It Means To Become An A.U.T.O.B.O.T.™ Leader

An A.U.T.O.B.O.T.™ leader does not chase AI trends.

They design AI deliberately.

They understand where automation belongs.
They demand data clarity.
They insist on accuracy.
They optimise before scaling.
They build for production.
They operate with discipline.
And only then do they transform.

This is leadership grounded in confidence, not hope.

Chapter Reflection

"AI does not replace leadership. It exposes the quality of it."

A.U.T.O.B.O.T. Assembly Progress: Piece 7 of 7
You have now completed the assembly of your Vertical AI A.U.T.O.B.O.T.™.

This final piece turns capability into leadership.

Your A.U.T.O.B.O.T.™ is now powering intelligent leadership.

This final piece turns capability into leadership.

This section contributes directly to your A.U.T.O. Pilot Blueprint, helping you apply the right type of AI to the right business problem.

Capture this clearly in your **A.U.T.O. Pilot Blueprint**. These decisions will form the foundation of your production-ready AI design.

AI does not remove responsibility. It increases it. Ownership must be clearly defined before deployment begins.

Reflect honestly:

→ Where could AI elevate decision-making rather than automate tasks
→ Which leadership behaviours must change to unlock AI's full value
→ How would your organisation look if confidence replaced hesitation

Write down one leadership decision that would change if AI outputs were fully trusted.

That decision is your **TRANSFORM** anchor.

You have removed repetition.
You have restored trust.
You have trained intelligence.
You have stabilised performance.
You have embedded accountability.
You have learned to operate AI safely.

Now you lead with it.

Conclusion

Becoming an A.U.T.O.B.O.T.™ Leader

> Leadership is about making others better as a result of your presence and making sure that impact lasts in your absence.
>
> ***- Satya Nadella***

The Vertical AI A.U.T.O.B.O.T.™

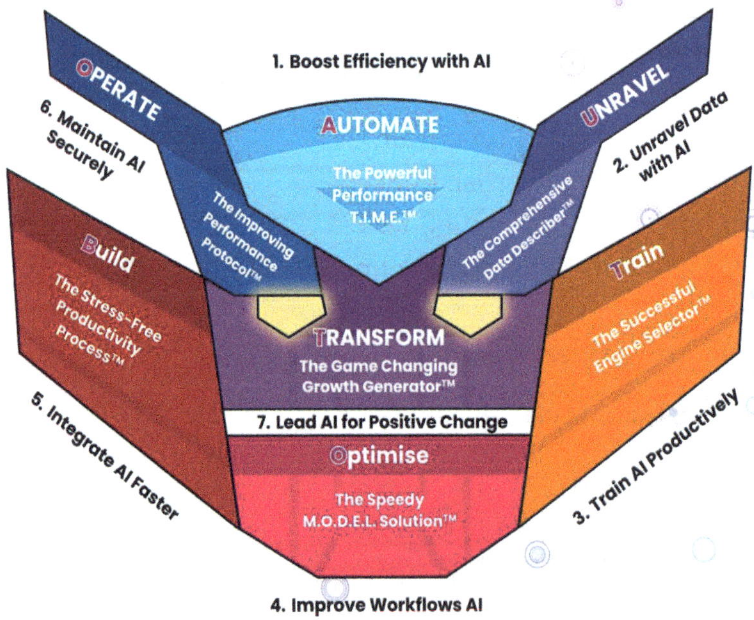

When I first entered investment banking in 1997, I was trained to operate inside systems.

Over time, I learned how to question them.
Then redesign them.
Then rebuild them.

What began as survival evolved into architecture.

This book has not been about technology.

It has been about responsibility.

From Chapter 1 to Chapter 4, we confronted the risks:

- Human robots
- Automation without control
- Confused AI adoption
- The compounding cost of getting it wrong

From Chapter 5 onward, you began assembling something deliberate.

You did not experiment blindly.
You built intentionally.

You:

→ Removed repetition.
→ Restored trust.
→ Earned accuracy.
→ Scaled without fragility.
→ Integrated with discipline.
→ Operated with governance.

And finally, prepared to transform.

That sequence matters.

Because transformation is not a leap.

It is the result of disciplined layers.

The Architecture at 50,000 Feet

Across every corporate, FinTech, founder, and SME environment I have worked in, one structural truth remains consistent:

Every successful Vertical AI system is built around a simple but powerful framework:

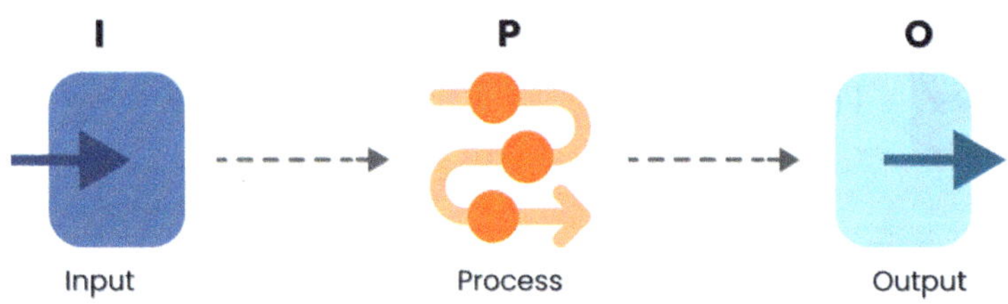

But the model's real strength lies not in the forward flow.

It is the human in the feedback loop.

Outputs must inform the process.
Process must refine input.

And humans must sit above the loop, not inside the noise.

Figure 9: The IPO Framework – Vertical AI at 50,000 Feet

At scale, every Vertical AI system should follow this structure:

→ **Input** – Unstructured, messy, real-world data
→ **Process** – Structured triage, tidying, training, testing, and human oversight inside a Large Domain Model
→ **Output** – Validations, automation, reconciliations, insights
→ **Human in The Loop** – Continuous learning from output back into process controlled by human

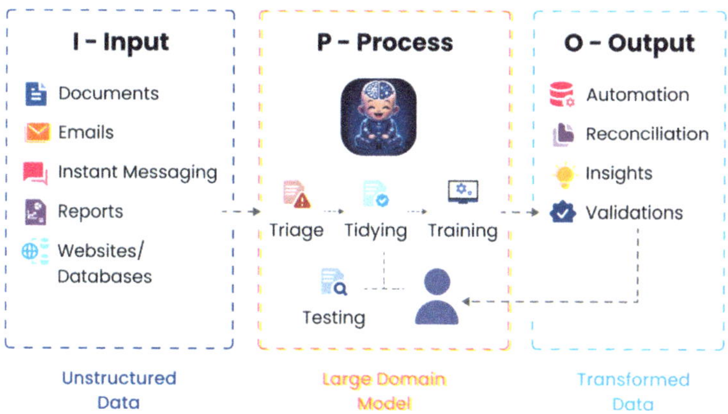

In my experience, this is how human learning works.

We receive information.
We process it.
We produce an outcome.
We adjust.

Vertical AI mirrors that same cognitive loop.

That is why the baby metaphor mattered earlier in this book.

You are not just installing tools.

You are building intelligence.

And intelligence only improves when feedback is deliberate.

The Full Assembly

You now hold the complete architecture of The Vertical AI A.U.T.O.B.O.T.™:

- AUTOMATE proves repetition can be removed
- UNRAVEL proves data can be trusted
- TRAIN proves accuracy can be achieved
- OPTIMISE proves performance can scale
- BUILD Integrate AI safely into live workflows.
- OPERATE Govern and monitor performance over time.

TRANSFORM Lead confidently with AI embedded into culture.

This is not hype.

It is a blueprint.

From Tasks To Judgement

Earlier in this book, I shared the metaphor of two babies.

One learns broadly.
One learns narrowly.

One explores language and creativity.
One learns domain precision and boundaries.

Both are powerful.

But only when trained properly.

Your organisation is no different.

Without structure, intelligence becomes noise.
Without governance, automation becomes fragile.
Without leadership, technology becomes theatre.

True AI maturity is not about adopting tools.

It is about designing systems where:

Machines execute.
Humans decide.
Leaders lead.

The Real Outcome

The outcome of this playbook is not efficiency alone.

It is something deeper.

- → People stop firefighting.
- → Decision-making speeds up without increasing risk.
- → Leaders trust the outputs in front of them.

Growth no longer depends on exhausting the best people in the room.

AI becomes boring.

And that is the highest compliment it can earn.

Because when systems are stable, humans can think.

When humans can think, they innovate.

When they innovate, they grow.

A Final Reflection

Look back at your organisation.

This section contributes directly to your A.U.T.O. Pilot Blueprint, helping you apply the right type of AI to the right business problem.

Capture this clearly in your **A.U.T.O. Pilot Blueprint**. These decisions will form the foundation of your production-ready AI design.

The organisations that succeed with AI will not be those that experiment the most, but those that execute with clarity, control, and consistency.

Where is repetition still stealing judgement?
Where does data still create hesitation?
Where are pilots still stuck in isolation?

Where is scale creating fragility?
Where is governance reactive rather than designed?

The answers to those questions are not problems.

They are starting points.

Becoming The Leader

An A.U.T.O.B.O.T.™ leader is not the loudest voice in the AI conversation.

They are the calmest.

They do not chase headlines.
They design foundations.
They do not automate for applause.
They automate for resilience.

They understand that AI is not about replacing people.

It is about protecting their capacity to think.

And they know that transformation is not a technology event.

It is a leadership decision.

If this book has done its job, you will not leave it excited.

You will leave it clear.

Clear about where to start.
Clear about what to build.
Clear about what to protect.

The future does not belong to organisations that experiment fastest.

It belongs to those who design best.

Over the next five years, artificial intelligence will quietly separate organisations into two groups.

Those who automated without architecture.

And those who designed with discipline.

The first will experience drift, reputational friction, and leadership fatigue.

The second will experience stability, clarity, and compounding advantage.

The difference will not be intelligence.

It will be responsibility.

AI will not replace leaders.

It will expose them.

And those who build with Automation, Control, and Intelligence in balance will not just survive the shift.

They will define it.

Build deliberately.

Lead calmly.

Design for confidence.

The next five years will not reward experimentation alone. They will reward disciplined builders.

Organisations that embed Automation, Control, and Intelligence in balance will reduce exception volumes by 30 to 40%, move high-value workflows into production in under 90 days, and free their best people from mechanical execution.

Others will remain stuck in pilot fatigue.

The difference will not be the budget.

It will be architecture.

You now have the blueprint.

Build deliberately.
Lead calmly.
Design for confidence.
And when others debate AI…

You will be operating it.

From Understanding to Execution

You have now completed what most organisations never fully achieve.

You have not just explored AI.

You have defined:

Your workflow
Your data
Your decision logic
Your risks
Your operating model
Your execution approach

And most importantly, you have captured this clearly in your **A.U.T.O. Pilot Blueprint**.

This Is Your Advantage

Most businesses remain stuck in:

Ideas
Pilots
Experiments

You now have something far more valuable.

You have the clarity required to move towards controlled, production-ready AI deployment.

Execution Is the Difference

Understanding AI is no longer the challenge.

Execution is.

Because moving from structured answers to a working AI agent requires:

Design that holds under real-world conditions

Integration across systems

Defined controls and governance

Operational discipline over time

This is where most organisations lose momentum.

What Comes Next

The next step is not more information.

It is structuring what you have already defined and moving it into execution.

You now have the inputs.

The outcome depends on how they are applied.

Final Thought

Most organisations will read about AI.

Few will act.

Fewer still will execute correctly.

The difference is not knowledge.

It is clarity, control, and discipline to move from idea to execution.

Appendix

ACI Principles and Skill Acronyms

> Don't reinvent the wheel. Vertical AI is the real deal.
>
> ***- Chetan Joshi***

The Vertical AI A.U.T.O.B.O.T.™ Playbook

The Vertical AI A.U.T.O.B.O.T.™ Playbook is a seven-pillar operating model designed to move organisations from experimentation to trusted production systems.

It is not a theory.

It is a progression.

Each pillar builds confidence before scale.

Each pillar protects judgement before automation.

Each pillar reinforces control before transformation.

The structure is deliberate.

The first four pillars form the **Pilot Phase**.

The final three pillars form the **Production Phase**.

Together, they ensure AI agents are not simply built but built responsibly.

Phase One: A.U.T.O. Pilot

The Pilot Phase

The Pilot Phase validates success criteria before AI reaches live production. This is where accuracy is earned, governance is tested, and outcomes are proven.

A – AUTOMATE

Boost efficiency with AI
Skill System: The Powerful Performance T.I.M.E.™.

Automation removes repetitive, deterministic work from humans so they can focus on judgement and leadership.

Automation operates under T.I.M.E.™:

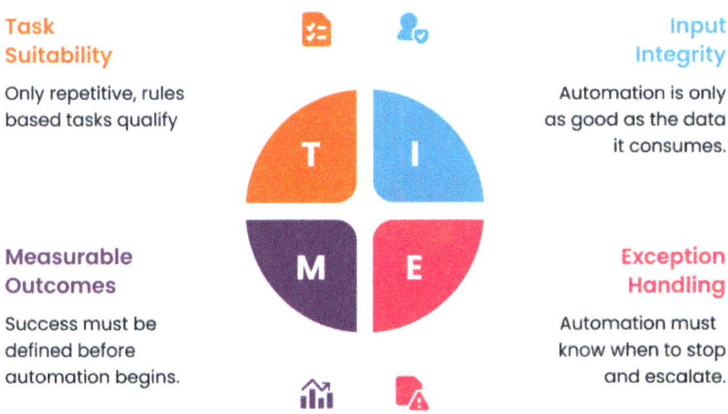

Automation is not about speed.
It is about controlled consistency

U – UNRAVEL

Unravel data with AI
Skill System: The Comprehensive Data Describer™

Unstructured information must be turned into trusted intelligence before AI can act reliably.

UNRAVEL operates under CCC:

- **C – Capture** All relevant data is captured at source, regardless of format.
- **C – Collate** Data is structured, normalised, and connected across systems.
- **C – Controls** Validation, lineage, and ownership are applied immediately.

Without clarity, there is no confidence.

Without confidence, there is no scale.

T – TRAIN

Train AI productively
Skill System: The Successful Engine Selector™

AI must demonstrate reliability before exposure to live environments.

TRAIN operates under T.T.T.T.:

Triage classify inputs and prioritise intelligently.

Tidying clean and standardise structured data

Training refine model behaviour within defined boundaries.

Testing validate performance under real-world scenarios

Accuracy earns trust.
Trust enables scale.

O – OPTIMISE

Improve workflows with AI
Skill System: The Speedy M.O.D.E.L. Solution™

Performance must remain stable as volume and complexity increase.

OPTIMISE operates under M.O.D.E.L.:

Measure – Monitor performance continuously.

Observe – Identify emerging patterns and risks.

Diagnose – Isolate root causes of instability.

Enhance – Implement controlled improvements.

Loop – Reinforce learning through structured feedback.

Optimisation without discipline creates fragility. Optimisation with measurement creates resilience.

Phase Two: B.O.T.

The Production Phase

The Production Phase embeds AI securely and sustainably into operational reality.

This is where responsibility replaces experimentation.

B – BUILD

Integrate AI faster

Skill System: The Stress-Free Productivity Process™

AI must move from pilot to production deliberately and safely.

BUILD operates under I.C.E.:

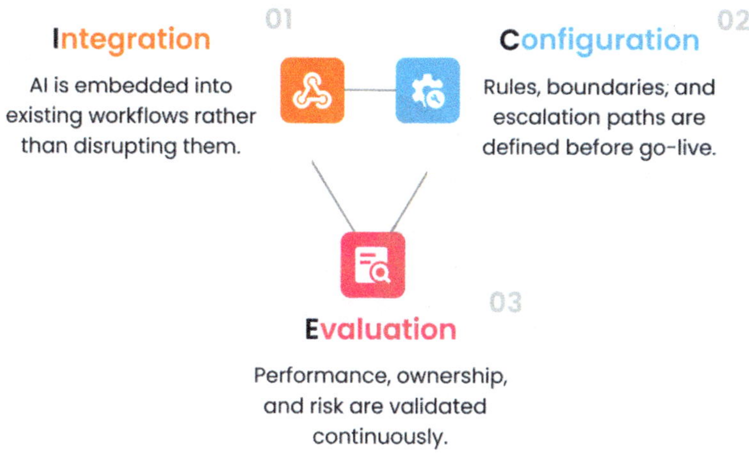

Pilots prove possibility.

Production proves responsibility.

O – OPERATE

Maintain AI securely

Skill System: The Improving Performance Protocol™

AI governance does not end at launch.

OPERATE operates under S.S.S.S.:

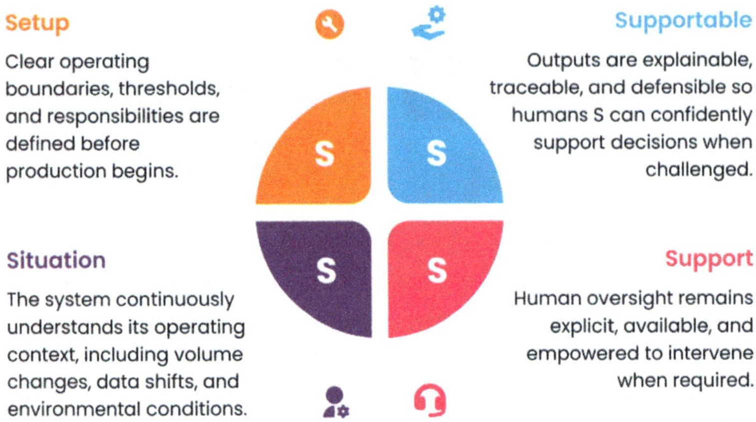

AI is not set and forget.

It is design and maintain.

T – TRANSFORM

Lead AI for positive change

Skill System: The Game Changing Growth Generator™

The final pillar elevates AI from operational tool to strategic advantage.

TRANSFORM operates under S.T.A.T.:

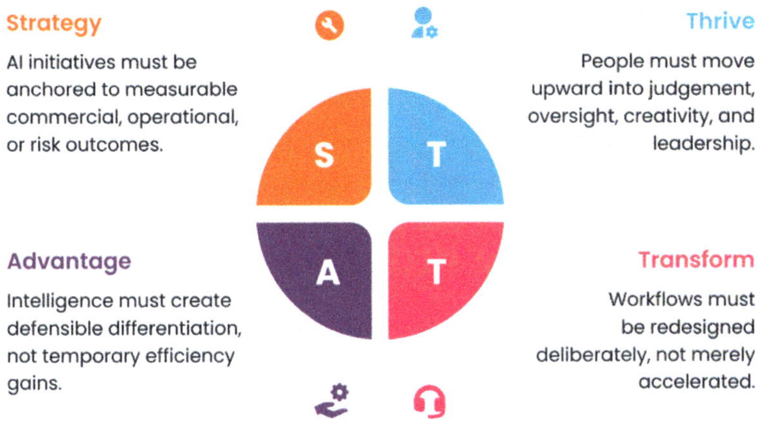

Transformation is not technology adoption.

It is organisational evolution.

The Governing Philosophy: ACI

The entire A.U.T.O.B.O.T.™ playbook sits within a wider discipline:

ACI – Automation, Control, Intelligence

This ordering is intentional.

Automation removes repetition.

Control protects trust and governance.

Intelligence enables superior decision-making.

Many organisations attempt to leap directly to Intelligence.

Without Automation and Control, Intelligence becomes noise.

ACI ensures maturity before scale.

Remove any one of the three, and AI becomes fragile.

Balance all three, and AI becomes dependable.

The Complete Progression

When applied sequentially, the playbook creates a disciplined evolution:

→ Remove repetition.
→ Create trusted data.
→ Prove accuracy.
→ Stabilise performance.
→ Integrate safely.
→ Govern continuously.
→ Transform deliberately.

This is the difference between:
AI projects and AI architecture.

One experiments.

The other endures.

Index

Use this index to quickly locate key concepts, frameworks, and execution steps across the Vertical AI A.U.T.O.B.O.T.™ Playbook.

About The Author

Chetan Joshi is a Vertical AI strategist, product architect, and business transformation leader with more than two decades of experience operating inside complex, regulated, and high -performance environments.

He began his career within banking and financial services, working in operational roles where precision was not optional, and accountability was personal.

Those early years shaped his philosophy. He saw firsthand how intelligent, capable people were forced to operate like human systems inside larger machines, reconciling, rekeying, validating, and checking.

The work was important. The repetition was exhausting.

Over time, one question became central to his career:

How do you remove human repetition without removing human judgement?

That question led him to the intersection of operations, technology, consulting, front office and artificial intelligence.

Chetan has worked with senior leaders across banking,

financial services, FinTech, and scaling growth businesses.

His focus has never been experimentation for its own sake. It has always been disciplined execution with building systems that function under pressure, stand up to scrutiny, and deliver measurable results.

He is the founder of **coglateral.ai**, an AI and automation growth consultancy that helps corporates, financial technology firms, founders, and small to medium enterprises design and implement Vertical AI systems that increase profitability, reduce operational risk, and create sustainable competitive advantage.

Unlike generic AI advisors who focus on tools and trends, Chetan specialises in domain-specific intelligence and production architecture. His work centres on structured, controllable, and auditable AI deployments with systems designed to operate inside real businesses, not just in presentations.

Through focused 90-day Vertical AI workflow mandates, he helps organisations move a single high-value operational process from pilot to controlled production. The goal is simple:

- Reduce exception volume.
- Free judgement capacity.

Increase confidence.

Establish a scalable foundation.

This approach reflects the philosophy of "**The Vertical AI A.U.T.O.B.O.T.™ Playbook**":

→ Automation removes friction.
→ Control builds trust.
→ Intelligence enables growth.

Through executive workshops, advisory mandates, and structured workflow deployments, he helps organisations move from AI noise to AI confidence, and from pilot fatigue to production discipline.

Chetan believes artificial intelligence should not replace human thinking. It should elevate it.

His work is dedicated to helping leaders move from uncertainty to clarity, from experimentation to architecture, and from reactive adoption to strategic advantage.

You Now Have the Playbook and the Blueprint

This is not a theoretical guide.

By this point, you have:

Defined your workflow

Structured your thinking

Captured your inputs clearly in your **A.U.T.O. Pilot Blueprint**.

You now have the foundation required to move forward. The Next Step Is Execution

The question is no longer what to build.

It is how to build it correctly, safely, and at speed.

Execution is where most AI initiatives fail.

Start Your Blueprint

Structure your inputs and move towards execution:

https://coglateral.ai/ai-start

What This Will Enable

By completing this step, you will be able to:

→ Align stakeholders internally
→ Define a production-ready AI workflow
→ Obtain accurate build or vendor pricing
→ Move confidently into execution

If You Choose to Go Further

Depending on your context, there are different pathways forward.

For Corporates and FinTech

Move from pilot to production with control.

Engage in a focused discovery process to:

→ Validate your highest-impact workflow
→ Pressure-test risk, controls, and architecture
→ Define a production-ready deployment plan

For Founders and SMEs

Move from idea to execution quickly.

Join a structured programme to:

→ Build your first AI agent
→ Launch a controlled workflow
→ Turn your blueprint into real business outcomes

Optional Guidance

If you would like support, you can request a session to:

→ Review your **A.U.T.O. Pilot Blueprint** inputs
→ Identify gaps and risks
→ Define your next execution step

www.linkedin.com/in/chetannjoshi/
Follow for real-world vertical AI strategy, frameworks, and execution insights

coglateral.ai/ai-start
Access your AI playbook builder, tools, and next steps

"The future won't be built by those who experiment with AI the fastest, but by those who operationalise it with control.

- Chetan Joshi

Made in the USA
Monee, IL
12 September 2026

62975588R00079